Columns by Georgia K. Hammack

Introduction by Gay Neale

Richard Hammack (publisher)
HammackRichard@gmail.com

Cover: Photo proof of Georgia Kilpatrick, probably taken while she
was a student at Westhampton College. Cover design by R. Hammack.

Hammack, Georgia K., 1928-2002.
    Columns / by Georgia K. Hammack; compiled by R. Hammack;
    introduction by Gay Neale. Edition 1.0. [Richmond, Va.]:
    R. Hammack, c2025.
    I. Title. II. Hammack, Richard H.
    PS3558.A4472 C65 2023   814.54

This work is licensed under the Creative Commons Attribution-
NonCommercial-NoDerivative 4.0 International License

Typeset in 11pt TeX Gyre Schola using PDFLaTeX

*To Georgia's grandchildren,
Adriana, Sage, Georgia and Paulina*

Contents

Acknowledgements	vi
Introduction	viii
Writing a Column for a Weekly Paper	1
Comparative Studies	6
Viola's Balloon	8
With the Heathens	11
Leaping Through Time	13
Boys and Blizzards	16
The Third Month	18
I Heard the Learned Birdwatcher...	20
Of Time and Children	23
At the End	26
Guineas	29
A Return	32
Beware of the Dog	38
Ahoy There, Mr. Bell	41
Doris the Hero	44
The Fourth of July	46
Trouble in the Ground	48
In the Summertime...	50

Summer Evenings	52
Gardening	54
Summer's End	57
For the Record	59
Getting it Straight	62
Canning Pickles and Jam	64
Once Upon A Time	67
Ponies	69
For the Picking...	72
Raw Materials	74
A Voting Record	76
A Question of Time	79
Time for the Feast	81
Giving Thanks	84
Communicating	87
Winter Mornings	89
Water Trouble	91
Moving the Millstone	94
Breaks	97
Yesteryear's Snows	99
A Modest Proposal	102
Perils	104

Acknowledgements

The columns in this book appeared between 1977 and 2002 in the South Hill Enterprise, and are reprinted here with its gracious permission. We also thank David Turner for painstakingly scanning and digitizing over 1200 columns.

Introduction

Georgia Hammack was always a lady, both in her life and as a writer. She had a delicacy and reserve that made whatever she did and wrote distinct and gracious, but she had a wicked sense of humor that slid into her innocent pieces like a bee into a flower. You will find that evident in the charming essays carefully compiled in this volume by her children.

Georgia grew up in a newspaper-owning family. She learned writing — proper, grammatical writing — from the cradle. She wrote these pieces as a regular column named Mscellaneous for the South Hill Enterprise weekly for over 25 years, a feat that always amazed me. They are gentle pieces about her home, nature, household routines, performances and exhibits she attended, and they often contained poems or quotes that struck her fancy. The last column she wrote was as fresh and winsome as her columns at their inception. Georgia also wrote delightfully witty plays, some of which won awards and were produced. She was interested in local history and wrote articles on several local figures for various publications. All of her writing was precise, clear, entertaining and lively.

We were friends for close to thirty years, and I enjoyed her companionship and good talk more than that of just about anyone I know. Our children grew up together and now are still good friends. For all those years, once or twice a month Georgia would come over in the afternoon, or I'd drop by her home, and we'd have a glass of wine and talk. We never talked about personal domestic matters; that was off-bounds for Georgia. Always the lady. We didn't even talk much about our grandchildren, although we were both very delighted to be so blessed. We would talk about trips we'd made, about events locally, about nature and the green world around us. But mostly we talked about writing and books. We exchanged manuscripts and were critical, supportive, enthusiastic and rueful together. Georgia liked short stories; I like novels, and we handed books back and forth. Her taste was excellent; her charm was extraordinary; her humor, water on a hot day. I miss her still.

Gay Neale   2023

Writing a Column for a Weekly Paper

"I've never understood," says essayist William Allen — and I haven't either — "those writers who say they'd write on a desert island with no hope of being read. For me, there needs to be a reader. I need to know that communication has taken place."

It's true, I think, that writers write, first, ultimately, and always, for themselves. But communication is vital. That's why I started writing a column for a weekly newspaper.

When you write a newspaper column, what you send in each week gets printed. Without exception. Without fail.

That's a terrific ego boost. And it helps when you have tangible evidence that people are actually reading what you write. In a small town, people stop you on the street and tell you they liked a column. They mention it at parties. Strangers even write you letters. It's great. I recommend it.

I can't really give tips about how to go about it. By definition, a personal essay column is the reflection of one person – his or her views, values, tastes, sense of humor, interests. Each column writer will be different. I can only tell you some ways I go about writing my column.

I started about 15 years ago when our daughter went to college and I decided I had some extra time for writing. I wrote three sample columns and mailed them to the editor of the South Hill Enterprise. I told him I could produce a column a week, for pay, and would he be interested?

I didn't hear for the longest time. Finally, I had a letter saying the Enterprise would be glad to print my column and would pay 50 cents a column inch.

I must say that I was very excited, even if I knew that fifty cents a column inch isn't much. Before I answered, though, I wrote to a friend who was writing a weekly column for a Connecticut newspaper and said — I can quote — "Please send me a postcard right away saying either yes or no. The question I want you to answer is: Considering the parsimony of editors and the vanity of writers, is 50 cents a column inch adequate pay for a weekly column?" She wrote back, by return mail, "Grab that 50 cents a column inch before the editor changes his mind."

So I did. Plainly, you don't write a column for a weekly newspaper for the money. I now receive 75 cents a column inch – and it's not very much. But writing the column is an enjoyable part of my life.

When I started the column I made a conscious decision — and told my editor — about things I would not write about; namely, national and international issues. I'm intensely interested in these, but I don't want to write about them. And I don't want to write about local political issues either.

Instead, I like to write about what Samuel Picketing, Jr., calls "the quiet byways of ordinary existence."

I've written a column, for instance, about learning to like okra (I cook it in the microwave oven and combine it with other vegetables). I wrote a column about the articles in magazines I always miss until I read about them in the next issue in indignant letters to the editor. I did another column about my husband going around the house at night with a flashlight to save electricity.

The last time I took my mother to the polls, I wrote about that. She was 85 and had voted in every presidential election since women first got the vote in 1920 when she was 21.

An easy category is What I Did On My Vacation. I hope these columns aren't the equivalent of subjecting friends to endless vacation slides. I try to be selective, to focus on an angle. I've written columns about castles in Spain, birds in the Pine Barrens of New Jersey, wilderness hiking in Colorado, a course on cosmology — the makeup of the universe — at an Elderhostel in Indianapolis.

I like writing book reviews. One review — in three parts over three weeks — was about Anne Fredor Scott's Invisible Women. She is head of Women's Studies at Duke. Not at all a militant feminist, she relates without bitterness and with extremely interesting details some of the contributions women made before they became "liberated."

Weekly newspapers are very good about announcing events. "The Tidewater Quartet will present a program for children at 10 a.m. on Wednesday at the Chase City Library" or "The poet Gwendolyn Brooks will speak at 7:30 Friday at St Paul's College." But very seldom do they send reporters to cover them. So there rush in I. I like reporting that the violinist in the string quartet wore a Lone Ranger mask when they played the William Tell overture, and that Gwendolyn Brooks said her mother told her — when at age 8 she showed her a poem she had written — "Oh, you're going to be a poet like Langston Hughes."

Likewise, I like reporting on events at our local community college. I think one of the most satisfying columns I ever wrote was when I read a notice on the college bulletin board that a nun from St. Mary's Hospital in Richmond was going to speak to student nurses, and I went out to listen. "Don't refer to a patient as the gall bladder in room 221," she cautioned, and she was especially perceptive in raising awareness about terminally ill patients. "There you are young and beautiful," she said, "but your patient is dying. Try to improve the quality of your patient's life." "Death," she said, "is about the quality of life...."

That column won a prize. It took about 20 minutes to write. I've spent as much as 20 hours on others.

Because I write for a small-town audience, I feel the need sometimes not to tell the whole truth. I can give two examples of what I mean.

I wrote a light, humorous column a few years ago about a workshop at a community college about Choosing Colors for Your Wardrobe. Maybe you are familiar with the Spring/Summer/Fall/Winter method of color selection: You decide — or have decided for you, by a color analyst for a fee — whether, with your skin, eyes, and hair coloring, you look better, say, in spring colors – pastels, pinks, greens — or in fall colors – golds and rusts. I forget what the summer colors are, but winter colors are dramatic — black, white. Anyway, you decide whether you're spring, summer, fall, or winter, and thereafter, unerringly, you can go to these colors in stores, neglecting all others, and come up unfailingly with something becoming. So far, so good. But the young woman who conducted the workshop — who was telling us how to always look our best — sat there the whole time she was talking and explaining, chewing gum. I don't care if she was spring/summer/fall/winter or all four – she looked dreadful. But in the column I didn't make this point. I didn't mention the gum. She is an area resident. I didn't want to say anything derogatory. Should I have made the point anyway?

The other example is a column about a workshop on recorder playing held in South Hill. The instructor was from Duke University and gives private and group lessons. He stutters. He had particular difficulty with "C's" and you can imagine how often he had trouble when talking about "recorders." I think a point could have been made in the column — graciously and without ridicule — about his courage and fortitude in teaching with this handicap, and the contrast could have been pointed out between his difficulty in speaking and his ease and skill in playing the end-blown flute. If I had been writing for The New Yorker, I would have done this. But in a small-town paper, I didn't. I didn't mention the stutter. I thought it might be interpreted as an unkindness. Was I wrong?

A talk given in July 1993 in Emporia, Virginia, at a meeting of the Traveler Chapter, Virginia Writers Club

Comparative Studies

My husband Jack has a way of going about the house at night with a flashlight. It saves electricity, he says.

I never thought much about this. In a long marriage one accepts the habits and idiosyncrasies of one's mate.

But our grown children, in the critical way of grown children, think it's hilarious.

"He looks like a burglar," said one.

"Only he makes more noise," said another.

Recently when they were all assembled here, they asked him, with feigned innocence, how much a kilowatt hour of electricity costs in this area. He went and got the electricity bills so they could figure it out.

They figured it out, and then went on to figure out, taking into consideration the cost of two D cell batteries, the comparative costs of burning an electric light and operating a flashlight.

Their happy conclusion: a flashlight costs 33 cents an hour and an 100-watt electric bulb costs only one cent.

"And the bulb gives more light!" they said triumphantly.

I have to say I was impressed by the mathematical calculations involved. We do have a son pursuing a doctorate in math.

Jack wasn't impressed, one way or the other.

"A flashlight is more convenient," he said.

It's easier, when you're in the habit of having one handy, to use it when going from room to room rather than having to fumble along the wall in the dark for the light switch. It goes without saying that in our frugal household lights aren't left burning in unoccupied rooms.

I don't use a flashlight myself, but I see the logic of it. And more than once, the flashlight Jack keeps by the bed has been a quick convenience when the less expensive electricity has gone off. In other words, I'm content to have a husband who wanders around the house at night with a flashlight.

One could do worse.

January 13, 1993

Viola's Balloon

When 21 second graders send you 21 letters and ask, among other things, how old you are and what grade you are in, it takes you back a little.

I am the happy recipient of 21 letters, written carefully in pencil on lined paper, because in December my husband sighted a balloon in a small tree while hunting in woods near our house. The balloon was deflated, and attached to it was a plastic bag. The next day I went with him to retrieve it, and, inside the bag was a postcard from Viola Allgood.

Viola is a second grader at Lewisville, N.C., near Winston-Salem. She and other members of Mrs. Jewel Harkey's class were studying weather. Would the finder of the mimeographed card please fill out the blanks and return? Viola had filled out blanks telling me about the weather in Lewisville and had signed her name. I wrote that the temperature in Lawrenceville on December 28 was 32 degrees, that there were patches of snow on the ground, and that it was windy. I signed my name in the space provided, gave my address and mailed it off.

I have since learned that of 27 helium balloons launched by an excited class on December 2, only the balloon that landed in our tree has been reported.

A Winston-Salem newspaper story describes the reaction of the children: "They waited and waited and still no word from the 27 balloons that were out there bobbing along the air currents, or snared in a tree, or torn and punctured in some forgotten creek or alley.

"Then came the card – all the way from Lawrenceville, Virginia. The children were excited, the teachers were astounded. A salesman from another store that stocked the balloons joked they were lucky if they got as far as Winston-Salem from Lewisville."

Then came the letters. Some of the children had learned to spell "delighted" for the occasion. One little boy gave up on it though, after writing "delig ..." The letters were literate, neat, and delightful. "Thank you, Georgia, for sending the weather card back. We were most delighted when Viola received it. The balloon went from Lewisville to Lawrenceville, Virginia – 166 miles. Wow!" "Where did you get the letter? We would like it if you wrote back. Some of us made weather instruments. How old are you?"

"We made weather instruments. My name is Melanie and I have a baby sister named Natalya. She giggles a lot. We hope you write us back."

"I am seven years old and I am in the second grade. How old are you and what grade are you in? The whole class wants to know where you got Viola's balloon. If you want to know what I look like, I have blonde hair, blue eyes and freckles. If you write back, please tell us what you look like.'"

"We were delighted to see your weather report. Thank you for sending it. You are a friend!"

"We would surely like you to write back. I am in the second grade. What grade are you in? We made a rain gauge, barometer, anemometer, and a weather vane. How old are you? We have finished with Norway and are now on pioneers."

Of course, with so many fetching invitations to write back, I couldn't refuse, and have mailed the class a letter giving detailed information about how the balloon was found, and also information about my age, hair color, and color of eyes.

February 18, 1981

With the Heathens

Sometimes on rainy February afternoons I think about my missionary and wonder if she were eaten by a crocodile.

I hope not. She didn't deserve such a fate, and I'm reasonably sure she escaped it.

In the Baptist Church of my childhood there used to be (and probably still are) organizations of little girls who studied foreign missions.

I can't recall the name of a single country. I remember images of jungles; rice paddies; travel by dugout canoe... sometimes a white cross in a clearing – the grave of a missionary, visited by devout, converted natives.

Once we gave a play (and I learned my lines overnight) about two enthusiastic missionaries talking about their work. The play lacked dramatic impact, but was a hit nevertheless.

My missionary came into the picture at a meeting at which we were all handed slips of paper with the name of a missionary on each. (My missionary!) Our teacher, at the conclusion of the meeting, was going to say a general prayer for missionary endeavors, and each little girl was then to give a special prayer mentioning her missionary by name.

I knew as soon as the plan was announced that I wasn't going to be happy about it. Saying lines in a play is one thing. Making up a prayer and saying it aloud is another.

I never said my prayer.

I shut my eyes tight, and scrouged down in my chair.

The teacher's prayer was interminable, then came the high piping voices of earnest little girls. Then silence.

"Is there anyone else to be prayed for?" the teacher asked.

I didn't say a word. My missionary went unprayed for. Visions of crocodiles flashed through my mind.

It was summer, and the group was meeting on the side porch of a neighbor's home. I could feel the coolness of the tiled floor on my toes, as I pulled my sandaled feet closer under my chair.

The silence lasted forever. I think the teacher asked again if there were another missionary who needed our prayers. My face was burning, but I trusted everyone else had eyes closed, too. Finally, knowing an impasse when she met one, the teacher tied things together with another prayer for all workers in the field, (apparently she hadn't a master list; my missionary wasn't mentioned by name.)

"You didn't pray for your missionary!" a friend whispered accusingly to me, poking me with her elbow, as the meeting ended and we got ready to leave.

I felt guilty for years.

Now, of course, I feel confident my missionary would have been forgiving. She might even have been amused.

I hope so. Her name is vanished from my mind forever balled up the slip of paper as soon as I received it and unobtrusively dropped it running home - but I'd like to think she had a sense of humor.

February 19, 1986

Leaping Through Time

ENJOY Leap-day while ye may.

In the year 2100; we won't have one.

That year is divisible by four — the criterion for deciding if a year leaps or not — but it's also a year ending in a hundred that is not divisible by 400.

This tedious calculation means that leap-day will be left out this year.

So decreed Pope Gregory, XIII in 1582 when, going on the advice of Aloysius Lilius, an astronomer of Naples, he reformed the calendar.

Put another way: Leap year which comes every four years is skipped every 100 years, unless the centurial year is divisible (evenly) by 400. The year 2000, accordingly, will be a leap year – or so I have it on good authority. My brains are rattling at this point.

The last time Leap-day was left out when ordinarily it would have been due was 1900. Perhaps people were so excited then about the beginning of a new century, they didn't particularly note the elimination of February 29.

I don't expect people will raise a hue and cry in 2100, either. But, then, who can predict the future?

In 1752, when England and other Protestant countries adopted the Gregorian or New Style calendar 170 years after Catholic countries had obeyed the Pope's decree, and

September 3 of that year officially became September 14, people poured out into the streets of London demanding that the king give them back their 11 days.

A change of only 10 days had been necessary in 1582 when the Pope announced that October 5 would be called October 15. There was grumbling then. Servants demanded full pay for the shortened month; employers refused.

The change in the calendar (painful though it was) was necessary because the Julian calendar, in effect since 47 B. C., had been rolling along through the centuries gradually becoming incorrect even with a leap year. Don't ask me how. It has something to do with the fact that the astronomers of Julius Caesar's day made a mistake of 11 minutes and 12 seconds in their calculations of how long it takes the earth to orbit the sun (or the sun to orbit the zodiac, as they thought in those unenlightened days).

It actually takes the earth 365 days, 5 hours, 48 minutes, and 46 seconds to go around the sun, in case you're interested. By the Middle Ages, those incorrect 11 minutes and 12 seconds had added up, so that dates on the calendar in some cases had lost their intended relation to solar events and to the seasons.

The modifications of the Gregorian calendar corrected this, and brought the calendar into such close exactitude with the solar year that there is only a difference of 26 seconds. This means, in case you want to worry about such things, that this will add up to a day in 3,323 years. I don't know what they will do about it then.

In the meantime, Leap-day, 1984 — and any Leap-day, for that matter — is worth celebrating. A whole extra day in the year. My. One ought to do something special with it. There ought to be some sort of national holiday, useless for commercial purposes, to commemorate the event.

The Japanese are great people for having festivals that are non-commercial times set aside to listen to insects' songs, or observe the position of stars. In the Western world, we could surely designate Leap-day as a day on which, as a friend put it, we could sit around and think about time.

This can be taken too far. I'd go distracted, myself, trying to figure out exactly why George Washington's birthday changed from February 11, 1751, on the old style calendar to February 22, 1752, on the new style. An addition of a whole year, in addition to those 11 days? Knowing that prior to 1752, the calendar in England and the colonies started on March 25 rather than January 1, doesn't really help me much.

Anyway, we ought to celebrate Leap-day in a special way.

Of course, the traditional prerogative of Leap-day, and Leap Year, traditional since the days of St. Patrick has been the right of women to propose marriage to men. In 1288 Scotland made it official: a law provided that every woman, no matter what her social class, had the right to propose during Leap Year, and if the man refused, he had to pay the lady a fine, unless he was already engaged to someone else. Other countries, in archaic days, passed similar laws.

In these feminist times, such dispensations may not be necessary.

Leap-day is, in fact, a good day to think about time – as measured by the ancient Egyptians (who had twelve 30-day months and five days of festivities at the end of year), and by the astronomers of Julius Caesar and Pope Gregory, and by the rest of us, to whom time is a mystery, in more ways than one.

February 29, 1984

Boys and Blizzards

It's nice to have a teenaged boy in the house when there's a blizzard outside, water pipes are freezing and the household is snowbound.

While daily, routine tasks are made more difficult for the people who do them daily and routinely, they take an aura of glamour for the snowbound teenager who is usually too busy with school and outside employment to participate.

Giving hay to the ponies is more fun for a boy when he has to trudge through knee-deep drifts, and bend his head against the blast to do it. The ponies, our teenager reported, greeted him with snorts of pleasure, tossing their manes which rattled with icicles.

Even taking food to the bird feeder is something of an adventure when snow is coming down hard and fast. When I suggested to the teenager that he put the food on a tray for ease in carrying, he replied, "Why don't you give me a towel to put over my arm?" However, because of him, the birds got their food when the morning was early, the wind was bitter, and I was still drinking my coffee. A teenaged boy is very good at prying frozen wood from the ground and bringing in snowy armfuls of wood.

He likes to scoop up buckets of snow and bring them in to be melted on the stove so dishes can be washed after the water in containers all about the kitchen has been depleted. If he felt any nostalgia for his childhood delight in eating snow ice-cream made by sprinkling Jello from the box onto a bowl of snow, he didn't mention it.

But his enjoyment of home-made soup in the middle of a snowy day was pleasant to behold.

The teenager's devotion to the car inspires him to go out with a shovel and tackle the driveway, while his parents either walk to work or stay contentedly inside. In the midst of the storm, before it was feasible to think of digging out, he walked a mile to work himself, to the one grocery store in the area that was open. "After I got there," he said laconically, "I heard over the radio that the chill factor was below zero." He said there were lots of customers. He got a ride back, bringing a few vital groceries for us.

On his trips to the driveway for digging-out operations, he clears the back porch and steps. He says, yes, he'll shake the snow off the boxwood so the branches won't break, and he'll open the door to the pump house so the sun can help thaw the engine.

Altogether, a very useful help in time of snow is a teen-aged boy.

What will we do next year when he's in college?

March 12, 1980

The Third Month

THE second time, this March, that we kept a window open overnight, the bird that the morning before had sung "truly, truly" outside the window before six o'clock didn't show up. I was disappointed. I had hoped to have music on schedule each morning henceforth, or for a while anyway. But birds, like March, are unpredictable.

That first morning I had gotten up and gone slowly to the window, not to alert the bird, and looked for it everywhere. Pinpointing a bird by its song, even in March when obscuring leaves aren't yet out, isn't easy. But finally, after several more "truly, truly's" I saw it, on a flowering shrub before the window; the shrub like the bird unidentified.

"What's that shrub?" visitors have frequently asked me. It will sometimes bloom (white) in January. I've never found out. And the bird was maddeningly unknown too, though I'm sure I've identified it, more than once, at our bird-feeder, by a book.

A sparrow. Of which there are many kinds. This one had a white throat. White throated sparrow, maybe? The light was still too dim to make out other distinguishing marks, stripe over the eye, spot or spots on chest.

Sparrows, so comparatively drab, compared, say, to blue and golden warblers or even to blue and black blue jays, redeem themselves, surprisingly, by song, which I can't recognize either or long remember.

But this one was singing, "truly, truly" or so it seemed, in the rich, heart wrenching way of a bird. I could see it open its beak and thrust forth its chest. So close and visible. A morning's delight. Several moments of pleasure.

This was beneath the south window. Our bedroom also has two east windows, good for viewing March sunrises. On the morning of the absence of the expected bird, through the nearer east window, I could see a band of blue clouds lying like a level-topped mountain.

Gradually the blue dispersed, first pushed out by a glow of red behind bare trees, then by streaks of yellow, and finally by the white and glaring sun.

Backed by the light, the elm tree outside the window had buds along its branches lit up like candle flames.

Say not that March is a cruel month. It has its compensations.

March 29, 1995

I Heard the Learned Birdwatcher . . .

I'VE had it with birds. I thought I liked birds as much as the next person, perhaps more than some, but after 10 days in Costa Rica with 17 members of the Audubon Society, it will be a while before I put binoculars to my eyes again.

Birders, as they call themselves, are a dedicated band. We had signed up for what was billed as a "nature" trip, with opportunities, the brochure said, to "explore" spectacular rain forests, national parks, jungles and isolated beaches of the country.

It turned out that just about all the persons on the trip except ourselves classified themselves as birders, and to them, "exploring" meant, for the most part, taking ten steps then spending ten minutes peering through binoculars exclaiming, "There's the Blue-footed booby!"

Sometimes we looked through binoculars, too, seeing, it must be stated, some beautiful and exotic birds, names largely unknown to us and unregretted, and sometimes we went off by ourselves at a less leisurely and less studious pace, but the cries of the birders remain in my head.

"Is that the gray-throated leaftosser?" they'd whisper, or the "tawny-throated leaftosser?"

"Oh, look!" (with a sharp intake of breath) "The scarlet-rumped tanager!" (This was one of the more easily identified birds.)

"There's the yellow-faced grass twit!" they cried once. If I hadn't seen this bird myself, with both the naked eye and binoculars, I would never have believed it existed.

Actually, the more serious the birder, the more restrained his remarks. He studied with an intent eye and a quiet mouth. Frequently, he looked with frank scorn at the more ignorant among us.

My husband, without binoculars, one morning sighted a bird they had all been eager to see, the keel-billed toucan, plainly sitting at the end of a dead limb. This was our most spectacular success as bird watchers.

I had been pleased, the first day, because I saw, following instructions from a helpful birder ("It's between the thick tree and the light trunked one, on that branch that goes off to the left at a 45 degree angle, just below those overhanging leaves at the 11 o'clock position") the mangrove humming bird. This is a humming bird, which unlike our eastern ruby throated one and like many other species of birds in Costa Rica, obligingly stays still instead of constantly flitting about. This is a great help.

The name, "mangrove humming bird" had been on a 16-page checklist that our outfitter had sent us prior to the trip. I stared at the list when it came. Over 544 birds. Could there be that many? Were we expected to see them all, and name them one by one?

I picked out at random, the name of the mangrove humming bird and, sure enough, I saw it on the very first day. I put a check by it and that was that.

None of the birders saw all 544 species, of course. Some of them saw over a hundred. They worked at it.

At night, they poured over their bird books (each birder had an average of four books) and compared them with the copious notes they had taken during the day. They made exhaustive lists. They asked the guide, and each other, what that small black bird with the white eye stripe, green chest, and blue back could be. There was a decided tendency to touch their own eyes, chests, and backs as they described the colors and characteristics of the birds. One birder said she was taking a computer course at a community college back home in Michigan, so she could computerize her bird records.

I, too, like to identify birds, to study bird books, and say to myself, "Now, did that bird have two wing stripes, or one?", but not all day long, for ten days straight.

The most tiring part of the pursuit of the bird, for my husband and me, was the time in the Monte Verde cloud forest when we all tiptoed out to see the courting dance of the blue-crested manakin. We stood motionless for 30 minutes in a slight clearing, the favored spot of the manakins, tiptoed cautiously forward another ten feet, then waited another 30 minutes. They never showed up. One Colorado gentleman with us, like us, was not a devout bird watcher. "I believe the blue-crested manaklns have already consummated their relationship," he concluded. We all went back to the lodge.

Now that we're home again, it's a relief to look casually out the window and see nothing but a common robin.

April 6, 1983

Of Time and Children

It's safe for non-quality time parents to come out of the closet now.

We've been lurking there for some time.

We're the mothers who for better or worse (and I freely concede it may have been worse) stayed home and weren't employed.

No one can convince me that this action makes us necessarily superior to working mothers.

At the same time, I'm not convinced that working mothers have a monopoly on 'quality time' with children. 'It's not the quantity of time you spend with children that's important,' has been the cry. 'It's the quality of the time.' The inference plainly is that these parents fill each shining moment they are with their children with happiness and light.

I have three children, and I can state unequivocally that I spent a lot of non-quality time with them. Time that was frustrating, vexatious, boring, difficult. ('Hell-time' is how one friend, a father, used to describe the hours between 5 o'clock - when the children are hungry, tired, and cross, and so is everybody else - and bed time - the children's.)

I'd go through it all again.

You can't have the sweet without the bitter.

That's what child experts are saying now; that it's impossible just to declare, 'Now we're going to sit down and have some quality time,' and always succeed; that the quantity of time is indeed important; it gives spontaneous opportunities for realizing those words so fashionable now: bonding, parenting.

"Did you know," I asked my husband recently, "that all those times when you played with the children, or took them on walks, you were 'bonding'?" "I thought I was 'parenting'," he replied.

Non-quality time parents know that what a parent may consider quality time doesn't always strike a child that way. When a parent has time for 'quality time,' the child may be busy with his own business, and doesn't want to be bothered, thank you.

You have to take quality time when you can get it, snatch it when you may, hold it to your chest and cherish it, and, as often as not, it comes not in planned and structured activities, but in sudden, unexpected moments, any time of day, or night, like a freely given gift, like a blessing.

Sometimes the very best times are just an awareness of each other, in a room, at a meal, outside in the yard... Non-quality time parents know also, all too well, that they have missed opportunities for 'quality time' by missing, too often, the wistfulness in a child's voice, or the wonder. By being snappish, impatient, unfair.

But children, we trust, forgive their parents. (And may we forgive those who trespass against us.)

And isn't non-quality time inevitable, and essential, after all?

Isn't it by sharing a measure of non-quality time with persons who love them dearly, that children learn to cope?

So non-quality time parents haven't been too impressed when others imply that time spent with their children is perpetually at a high quality peak. According to a recent Niki Scott column, working women, too, some of them, are now admitting that it isn't always so.

Good. The truth will get out, and the truth will make us free.

Free to admit, that for both working and nonworking parents, life has few things to offer more rewarding and precious than quality time with children, but that it can't always be arranged, like meals, on a schedule, or called for on demand.

April 17, 1985

At the End

A PERSON who is dying doesn't need to be told it's God's holy will, a nun told area student nurses recently — the patient needs to feel that those taking care of her, care for her as a person.

"The greatest gift you can give a dying person is yourself," Sister Elizabeth Durney said. A capable looking woman who wore modern attire, a black suit with soft lavender blouse, she spoke on "Aging and Dying" at a morning workshop April 13 at the Christanna campus of Southside Virginia Community College. Her talk was sponsored by the nursing department of the college.

Sister Elizabeth is a member of the Sisters of Bon Secours (Kindly Care), Richmond, who own and operate St. Mary's and St John's Hospitals.

Nurses should be aware, she said, not only of the needs and emotions of a young patient facing an untimely death, but of the needs and emotions of elderly persons who are dying.

She read to the audience a poem written for her by a young woman, no longer living. It expressed gratitude for Sister Elizabeth's care, and ended with the wish that she could help her.

"My time is coming, too," said the white haired nun.

"Please treat with reverence the things I tell you that dying people have told me," she said. "It's a gift to me from people at a special time in their lives."

Sister Elizabeth in 1975 started the pastoral care department at St. Mary's Hospital. She is now director of Bon Secours Chez Vous ("Kindly Care in Your Home"), a program begun in 1982 to aid well elderly persons in their homes.

She had few set rules or do's and don'ts for dealing with the terminally ill.

She did urge nurses to always know and use the patient's name. "For goodness sakes, don't refer to the gall bladder in room 204." (To remind nurses that each patient is a unique person, she quoted Isaiah: "I have called you by name, and you are mine, and I love you.") In answer to a question, she said no, a nurse should never let a difficult, trying patient know that her behavior is getting her down. "If it's bothering you too much, you need help yourself. You could alleviate your feelings by talking about it to another nurse, or a friend. But the patient doesn't need this additional burden."

In brief, poignant remarks Sister Elizabeth conveyed some of the anxieties and fears felt by dying persons. "A woman may feel her husband won't be able to cope emotionally with her death, and her absence — and what will become of the kids? A patient may experience anger because the nurse caring for her is young and beautiful, and she is dying... An elderly patient may feel isolated, lonely..."

Many times, she said, the dying person may want someone just to listen when he talks. "If a person doesn't want to talk, touch is a wonderful thing."

She urged nurses to think of how they themselves react to death, not only of a friend or family member, but to other "deaths" within their lives: the loss of a job, separation, divorce. She said that how they deal with these situations may give insights into dealing with death.

"Caring must come from within," Sister Elizabeth said. "I can't tell you what to do, or what to say. Try to make each day more special and meaningful for the dying patient. Try to enhance the quality of life. Death is about quality of life..."

April 25, 1984

Guineas

GUINEAS! people frequently say when they come to our yard. "You have guineas." And, as likely as not, there'll be an enchanted, nostalgic look on their faces.

"Why, my mother used to raise guineas," they'll say – or an aunt or a grandmother.

There is something about these homely yet exotic looking birds that's comforting and reassuring to many people. I think they seem to be more appealing, for instance, than peacocks, though Flannery O'Connor whose non-fiction I like so much more than her short stories has an intriguing essay about the peacocks she used to keep at her home in Georgia, and I don't mean to malign them. But guineas just seem more satisfactory, somehow less show-offy, more basic, more fundamental.

We only have two. We started off with five some years ago, imported from a friend, for the purpose of keeping down ticks, which they have done. The number has wavered, been reenforced, and now settled at a pair. They wander about at large without being bothersome and we've never had to feed them. They don't bother the garden either.

They peck about with staccato movements of their small, ridiculous heads, and come running, like little old ladies holding up long skirts, when we drive up in the car. At first we thought this was true affection, and were touched, until we realized that they like to look at their reflections in the hub cap. I don't think this is vanity (as it would be fun to imagine, with peacocks), but gregariousness. They probably think the reflections are more birds of a feather. No one ever accused a guinea of being overly bright.

They have other virtues though. Their soft, dark gray feathers, speckled with white, on the oddly oblong-shaped bodies, make a pleasant sight... against lush green grass, under an apple tree ... And the clucking of the hens is unusually melodious and sweet. It reminds me of a phrase of the 18th century naturalist, Gilbert White, "A mummuration of birds". This music is one thing people like most about guineas, I think.

Of course they can make a dreadful racket, too, that has to be heard to be believed – incessant, rattlely, frenzied, high pitched, and indignant. The late Dr. Robert Tynes of Lawrenceville used to like to tell a story about a meticulous golfer at the old Brunswick Country Club on old Rt. 46, who, just as he was concentrating on a stroke, would be put off by the sudden clamor and uproar of the guineas on a farm across the road.

This noise has gained guineas a reputation for being "better than a watchdog", and there are innumerable and ancient stores about guineas alerting Caesar's camp, or a frontier village, about an impending attack. But I'd hate to have to depend on it. Our guineas usually take most intruders to their domain very calmly. However our setter dog has high respect for their pecking ability. They have only to given her a hard look, and she'll retreat hastily, even giving up her dinner to them, if we don't intervene.

Another thing people like about guineas is the chicks. Visitors keep telling us how pretty and appealing they are. We've never had chicks. We've been told that guineas are notoriously scatterbrained parents, hiding their nests so thoroughly they forget where they put them themselves, or dropping eggs carelessly about.

We once found an egg on the back porch, just in time for breakfast. (Fortunately, the guineas maintain a half-wild status, and don't come on the porch very often.) And one evening the children came in, giggling, with an egg they said they'd found under the oak tree where the guineas were roosting. (The eggs are smaller than a chicken egg, and have a much harder shell).

But I think it would be fun to have some chicks around. And I have an idea, too, that there would be lots of people around who'd gladly offer to take some of them off our hands.

May 18, 1977

A Return

WHEN, during World War II, I studied high school French, we used a reader called Le Beau Pays de France (the beautiful country of France). It has taken me a long time to actually get to France, and indeed it is a beautiful country.

I didn't want to leave after a recent stay of six days in northeastern France, in a village of red tiled roofs, steep hillside streets, flowers in window boxes, and a view everywhere of the surrounding, blue-green Vosges mountains.

This was Fremifontaine; population, 350.

My husband Jack was there during World War II.

This spring, our daughter Amy who had majored in French at college, leafed through maps, located the village, found out that it has a "gite" (a lodging place listed with the French government), made reservations and travel plans, and with her husband David along, acted as our translator when Jack returned with me.

We had thought the return visit would be a personal pilgrimage, of no especial interest to anyone but ourselves. Instead, Jack found himself an instant celebrity.

"Ici? Ici?" ("You were here? Here?") cried our hostess excitedly, when Amy told her Jack had fought at Fremifontaine. Her family had lived in a basement for over three weeks during the fighting.

"He liberated us!" she called to a neighbor, waving toward Jack as she mounted the steps to show us our apartment.

Word quickly spread. The next day when we went, for a promised tour of the village, to our hosts' home (they are Monsieur and Madame Paul Bussi), neighbors and a relative were there. One neighbor, it turned out, is a correspondent for a city newspaper; he wanted a picture and an interview. Another showed up rattling a vintage GI plate and canteen. "Maybe these were yours?" she suggested playfully? The relative (a cousin of Madame Bussi), was, carrying a book, heavily underlined, about the Vosges campaign. Now with a grey mustache, he had been ten years old when Fremifontaine was occupied by the Germans in 1944. The others had been a little older, from 12 to 17. They all talked about the war as if it happened yesterday.

The cousin and Monsieur Bussi took us in the car and showed us remains of German and American foxholes in nearby woods. (Beautiful woods, of fir and beech where we later took long walks.) Jack was the first American soldier they knew of who had come back to the village. They pointed out homes that had been damaged by artillery shells, the older homes dating back to the 17th century, when the village was rebuilt after destruction in the Thirty Years War. They tried to determine (not conclusively) which had been the barn in which Jack's platoon had herded 20 German prisoners (Jack recalls taking seven prisoners himself); and, going by a map Jack sketched, found the road (now just a lane) down which Jack had marched into the village. Jack was with the 180th Regiment of the 45th (Thunderbird) Infantry Division.

He hadn't been with the first members of the regiment who entered Fremifontaine on October 2, 1944. When he arrived, Oct. 4, his platoon was told by intelligence that the village was safe in American hands. Pockets of resistance remained, however. The platoon was suddenly fired upon by Germans who materialized in the field between the road and the village. As Jack told his French interviewer, this was the first time since he had arrived in Europe in August 1944, that he heard bullets whistling by his head.

After capturing the Germans, the platoon slept in a field that night before going on to further fighting in the mountains.

Madame Bussi had been 15 when the Germans occupied the village September 29, 1944. Soldiers took over the bedrooms of her house forcing her parents and her to the basement where a neighboring family of four also retreated.

This is the house where she and Monsieur Bussi now live. They showed us the stone walled, two room basement; dark, small, built in the 17th century. Now, they store wine there, and potatoes and home canned vegetables.

Even after the Americans came, and the Germans had vacated the house, and then withdrawn to the hills, the group remained in the basement as artillery shelling waged between both sides. During the day, Madame Bussi told us, they would go out, an hour or two at a time as shelling permitted, to care for the farm animals. Sometimes they would be preparing meals in the kitchen, when shell fire would make them grab the food and dash for the basement.

"It wasn't all bad." said Monsieur Bussi, who had a similar experience in another village. "We prayed, told stories."

As fighting progressed and the front wavered back and forth, both German and American casualties were high.

Madame Bussi's home received five hits from shells. A nearby house (the home of the wife of the journalist) was destroyed by American shell fire.

But, "We were happy to see the liberators, "Madame Bussi said. "We wanted to ring the church bells, put out flags." but the French army "said no. The Germans would come back and burn the village down."

Madame Bussi remembers her first sight of the American soldiers. "One evening, I saw soldiers, but they weren't wearing green uniforms. They were Americans!" One day, she ran out to see an American tank. As shelling started, "the soldier popped down into the tank. I ran back to the basement."

Four men of the village were taken by the Germans to the concentration camp at Dachau, and only one came back. This survivor lived until only a few years ago. Madame Bussi showed us his grave in the village churchyard.

The director of the American Military Cemetery and Memorial at nearby Epinal, which we visited, pointed out to us that people of northeastern France experienced more direct contact with war than the people of Normandy who only saw fighting at first hand at the time of the Allied invasion. Northeastern France also saw fighting in the First World War. (On the living room wall of the Bussi home are photographs of two uncles killed at Verdun.) Then, earlier, there had been the Franco-Prussian War, 1870-1871. At Epinal we saw a statue to the victims. But, said Monsieur Bussi philosophically, "Wars are started by politicians. The German people are as nice as we are."

Our stay at Fremifontaine was peaceful. By our lodging, black and white cows, in a long lush pasture, walked sedately to and fro (as if talking of Michelangelo). Lilac and apple trees bloomed in the yard. Church bells rang. (Electronically controlled, we learned.) We went each morning to the village bakery for pastries and the obligatory, unwrapped loaf of French bread. We drove to larger communities for complicated French meals. We visited a castle.

Often, we encountered our hosts. One morning they were planting potatoes in a field they own not far from their house, their car parked at the edge of the field, Madame Bussi in a neat, dark blue dress. The day we left, Monsieur Bussi was feeding lengths of wood into a circular saw he'd put up in the yard. When we visited the village church, Madame Bussi showed us hand embroidered altar linens that she had ironed for a Sunday service.

Monsieur Bussi is a retired carpenter who had been self employed. After their two children grew up, the couple decided to operate a "gite" as a retirement investment. Built next to their home, it has the same beige masonry walls, red tile roof, and brown wooden shutters.

The Bussis advertise through an English agency, and in 21 years have had guests from England, Germany, Belgium and America, as well as French vacationers who traditionally vacation in July and August. A group of agricultural students, attending a work-study program, moved into the "gite's" other apartment, next to ours, before we left.

Most people in the village, Madame and Monsieur Bussi told us, have lived there for generations, but in a pattern also familiar in rural Virginia, children now leave to live in other places, and many residents work elsewhere. Traditional occupations were farming and working in the forests.

Those beautiful forests, mostly government owned, owe their beauty largely to strict regulations by the French government, mandating careful harvesting and forbidding clear-cutting. In forests owned by the village, firewood is reserved for local inhabitants who can buy it at the town hall. On the evening set aside for the picture taking and interview, we met again at Monsieur and Madame Bussi's home. The journalist's wife was there (her hair damp from swimming in a pool at a nearby town) and the cousin, still with his book. In the French manner we sat around a table. Amy translated ably, but even if I hadn't understood a word, I would have enjoyed the voluble talk flowing back and forth, with gestures and laughter.

Madame Bussi brought out glasses and her husband opened two bottles of champagne. "Sante!" (Health!) we exclaimed, clicking glasses.

The cousin leaned far across the table to click Jack's glass. "Sante au liberateur!" (Health to the liberator!) he said.

June 3, 1998

Beware of the Dog

Being of a sympathetic nature, I sometimes wonder how dogs must feel when they are tied or penned by signs saying "Vicious Dog", "Bad Dog" or the like.

After all, psychologists warn us that if we "put labels" on children, they frequently act accordingly. Experiments, they say, have shown that teachers act differently toward students they have been told (falsely, by the experimenters) are "superior" – and that the children respond with raised levels of achievement. Conversely, superior students, labeled "below average", responding to unconsciously slanted attitudes, fail to meet their potential.

There's something to this, surely – but not too much, I would think (in my backward way).

However, it's true that all the dogs I ever met by "Beware of the Dog" signs lived up to their labels. Whether they acquired their characters because of their signs, or (as I suspect) were Rotten Ralphies to begin with, I'm not prepared to say. And how the dog feels about his sign, whether he's rather proud of it or nurses hurt feelings, is, when you come down to it, idle conjecture.

It's true that all dogs don't look as if they match their labels. I once encountered an attractive wire haired terrier, his chin poised pensively on his crossed forepaws as he lay chained to his sign, "Cross Dog", who looked anything but cross. In a forgetful moment, though, I got too close, and he ran like a bolt of lightning for my ankles, looking, indeed extremely vexed.

Another time my husband, visiting in a home, was held captive in his chair by a large German Shepherd who fawned and wagged his tail as long as Jack remained seated, even nuzzling fondly against his knees. All changed, however, to snarls, growls and bared teeth, the moment he rose to leave – whereupon he sat down hastily again until someone who could "manage the dog" was summoned. (This dog was labeled "Vicious".)

I thought about all this the other day because all of us were unexpectedly held hostage in our home for about an hour by a "Bad Dog", so called, who bounded, baying, around the house like the Hound of the Baskervilles, to hurl himself first against the front door and then the back. He was an exceedingly large and dark German Shepherd and when he stood on two legs, pawing at the screen door, the expression, "darkened the threshold" was never truer.

Our younger son recognized him as the "Bad Dog" (his pen is so labeled) who is kept as a guard for a trailer park near us. In fact he had just come from a neighbor's where the dog's owner, (our friend, Valerie Doxtater) has come, looking for the dog, and warning that he might bite. (The dog had gotten out somehow during a storm – I forget the complicated details, but the pen is safe, and escape, again, unlikely.) Anyway it took us a while to contact Valerie, and it was a strange feeling to eat supper listening to ferocious bursts of barking and knowing we were hostages in our own house.

The guineas, ignoring their "label" as watchdogs, were unperturbed, but our timid setter was beside herself. At one point, when the German Shepherd was on the front porch, and we thought, fairly quiescent, we cautiously opened the back door and let our setter slip in. She streaked upstairs (hitherto, unknown territory to her) and jumped in a bunk bed. Not a moment too soon, for the Bad Dog, enraged, tore to the back door almost before we had time to shut it. We called our other son who was visiting a friend and told him not to get out of the car when he came home unless we first signaled to him that all was safe.

And soon, all was, for Valerie showed up; and the dog docilely enough, after some coaxing and sweet words (the psychologists, I suppose, would claim a point there) hopped into the car, and they drove away.

It had never felt sweeter to open the front door and step outside.

June 29, 1977

Ahoy There, Mr. Bell

WHEN a representative of a telephone company calls to conduct a survey, I believe in telling it straight.

"Is this a good time for you to talk?" a syrupy female voice inquired the other night, at dinner time, after stating her purpose.

"Not really," I said, "but go ahead." At least it wasn't a request for funds for a worthy cause, which no matter how worthy, we automatically turn down if it comes via telephone.

"How often do you use your telephone?" she next inquired.

"As little as possible," I said.

How true. As a child I shared the misgivings of our "house girl" Nettie, who held the telephone as if she expected it to explode any minute. I always let someone else answer it, when it rang. I'm mystified now when parents tell me their children spend hours on the phone. I went like a galley slave when the call was for me. If it was ever absolutely necessary for me to place a call — if I'd forgotten an arithmetic assignment, for example — I told "Central" the number reluctantly and then raced through the conversation. If a grown-up answered the phone I never said anything but "MayIspeaktoMaryStuart?"' (Mary Stuart, on the other hand, always exchanged pleasantries with my mother or aunt, prompting them to say what nice manners she had.)

My telephone manner, to this day, is hurried and uneasy.

"How do you feel," the telephone representative asked, "when you miss an important message?" "I'm delighted," I told her.

She gave a little trill of laughter. It's no laughing matter. It's my experience that important messages that come over the phone interrupting your dinner or calling you from far reaches of the yard are seldom that important. If they are, and you miss them, the caller will call back later.

"Do you receive more calls than you place?" she asked.

"Yes," I said. She might have surmised that, I thought.

I do make calls. The telephone can be a useful tool, but other people consider it more useful than I do. She didn't ask if I socialize over the phone – make calls just to talk. I don't know what I would have said if she had, so strong is my aversion to this horror.

Her next comment was a sales pitch. She first ascertained that yes, most of my long distance calls are to the same numbers, to family members and relatives. "Would you be interested in a quick-call system," she asked, "enabling you to call easily and quickly the numbers you use most often..."

"How much does it cost?" I interrupted.

"Two dollars and fifty cents a month."

"I'm not interested."

"May I ask why?" She was very polite.

"I can dial those numbers quickly enough as it is," I said. "I'm not in that big a hurry. Especially for $2.50 a month."

"But that's only eight cents a day."

"Yes, but I don't make long distance calls every day."

Indeed I don't. I invest from time to time in a 25 cent stamp, and record my thoughts for posterity. Posterity may little note or long remember what I write, but I still think letter writing is an art that should be practiced more often.

The representative gave up and thanked me nicely for my time.

I have to admit we have a daughter who calls occasionally just to talk. (The telephone messages of our sons are limited to, "Happy Mother's Day," or "Okay if I come down on Friday and bring Liz?")

My husband, reading on the sofa, is always restless during our daughter's calls.

"Tell Amy that's a long distance call," he says, after three minutes.

"I'm paying for it, Daddy," she responds.

"It's still a long distance call," he says indignantly.

That's the way I feel about it, exactly.

June 28, 1999

Doris the Hero

We haven't seen the first hoof print by a deer in our garden this season. Last year they ate our snaps like crazy.

The reason for this abstinence is our dog. Doris the hero.

We moved her dog house to the garden area, and every night chain her there. It may be too early to claim permanent success, but we rejoice in free growing vegetables, not chomped off.

Doris, a white pointer, knows our pleasure.

She looks modest when we congratulate her, but we think this has given her a new lease on life. A sense of purpose. A job.

Dogs are smart. She must have sensed our disappointment in past years at her lack of distinction as a hunting dog. Now we forgive this transgression.

When Doris first caught on to the fact that she was going to be dispatched to the garden every night, she put up a token protest. She'd run and hide in the lilac bushes.

But she was easy to catch there, and once the leash was attached to her collar, she went with us straight to her post, tail tucked, but resigned.

Now we just give her a look, and she bounds off, tail wagging, and hops in her house.

We don't trust her enough, yet, to leave her there unchained, but who knows? Maybe her sense of responsibility will reach that point.

As it is, she starts barking around five in the morning when my husband gets up. Enough is enough, she says, and he releases her. She snorts and prances, sneezes and cavorts.

We're happy to have such a useful animal, performing a valuable purpose for us.

And no question about it, garden-watching has increased Doris's self-esteem.

We recommend it to other dogs in the land.

June 21, 1989

The Fourth of July

GROWING UP in the South during the Depression, I never experienced much in the way of a July Fourth celebration. It was considered something of a Yankee celebration then, and I suppose nobody had the money anyway for firecrackers and other fireworks. If we did, we saved them for Christmas.

But I like the idea of an old fashioned July Fourth celebration – horse races, maybe bands playing in circular stands in parks; parades with prancing horses down small town streets, and speeches (if it can't be avoided) by politicians from flag-draped outdoor platforms.

Actually, I think once during the 30's, Lawrenceville did have a Fourth of July parade. I don't know how it came about, and there weren't any prancing horses (horses during the Depression were used on the farm and didn't feel like prancing), but there was a marching band from Martinsville as the great attraction — advertised weeks in advance — and what was more, the band had twin majorettes. The picture of two brunette girls, undeniably twins, though not identical, appeared time and time again in the "Brunswick Times-Gazette" prior to the event, with the caption, "The Only Twin Majorettes in the World." I wonder now, idly, if this record has been broken since, but, then, I was absolutely stunned that celebrities of such caliber were coming to Lawrenceville.

The parade went off very well as I recall, twin majorettes and all, with great fanfare and excitement on an extremely hot, dry day. But it didn't end up as a yearly practice. It did stir up, though, some talk about the possibility of Lawrenceville High School having a marching band. One girl announced she wanted to play the piano, and in the glee of envisioning her playing a piano being wheeled down the street with herself following on the wheeled piano stool, the idea of a band caught fire for a while, then died down. This was, after all, the Depression. I don't know how Martinsville managed a band, nor what future fame awaited the twin majorettes.

I don't remember any other public Fourth of July celebrations from those days, or even doing anything unusual in the way of private celebrating – except once eating watermelon at a cabin on York River, and another time riding a white mule, Pearl, through town with my friend Josephine Bostick on a 17-hand horse in what wasn't intended as a parade at all. It was just a ride, but on a busy Saturday attracted a lot of attention, Josephine could give that mule a signal and she'd kick.

And now that I think about it, and am completely truthful about the matter — as much as I like — in the abstract, the idea of a big, traditional, public July Fourth celebration, I probably wouldn't go if one were offered here.

July is a busy month, and the Fourth is no exception. Rather than be in a crowd, I'd probably want to stay home and work in the garden.

That's as good a way as any to celebrate the Declaration of Independence – and life, liberty and the pursuit of happiness.

July 4, 1979

Trouble in the Ground

Two of the biggest men I ever saw, and a smaller fellow with a smile like an elf's, came out to our house the other day to see what was wrong with our well.

We are always having well trouble.

Our old hand-dug, stone lined well, in use for nearly a century, developed a high bacterial count. The well we had bored to replace it went dry. A drilled well, deeper and surer, was the next step.

Our landscape is dotted with wells.

And now no water was coming out of the spigots when I arrived home in the midst of a storm that had toppled a tree, bent the tomato plants, and sent rainwater driving under window sills to form puddles on the bedroom floors.

The trio of workmen from our well company, responding the next day to my call, took the cover off the well and decreed that nothing was wrong with the state-of-the-art submersible pump there (the pumps we have had).

"I don't guess lightning struck a pipe in the ground," said one of the three.

"Double, double toil and trouble," thought I.

Lightning had indeed struck a pipe in the ground. It had struck a tree and traveled, in the way of lightning, through the roots straight to the pipe. This is a first in our trouble with wells.

It had taken the men a while to locate the strike. In tones I could hear from the house they called to each other as they scouted the yard looking for water seeping up from the ground. "I got it! Here it is!" one called. They set to work with shovels, ("Look at all them roots") and then went and got a backhoe. ("A little bit more over this way!")

High drama, all of it.

"Look at this pipe" they said to me finally. They handed me two sections, ragged and shattered. I kept them to show to the insurance company.

All was not over yet. The pipeline was comparatively easy to repair, but the backhoe showed signs of getting stuck in the mud. The fellow with the elflike smile shook his head wonderingly. In mudcaked boots, the workmen decided to come back on a drier day and finish the job of covering up the hole and trench.

So much for our current well trouble. The aftermath is that bits of grit and dirt from the muddy water that first came coursing through the pipes have messed up every faucet and toilet in the house and visits from our plumber, likely to be prolonged, are scheduled.

In the midst of it all, I've been eyeing the wellhouse that covers our antique well. Visitors have sometimes thought the wellhouse was a gazebo or summerhouse, with its peaked roof and latticework over the siding. But it's always been packed with well paraphernalia.

Now maybe its day has come. We could remove the old hand pump (maybe the Brunswick County Museum would want it), take out other assorted equipment from various epochs, put in a window or two, install Chippendale benches or something more comfortable, and could retreat there for peace in stressful moments.

Such as times when things go wrong with our well.

July 8, 1992

In the Summertime...

Does a snake feel cooler when it sheds its skin?

Is it cool within the insulating walls of a hornet's nest?

Hot weather drives me to questions like these.

I don't need newspaper or TV warnings to stay out of the sun when our porch thermometer registers 98 degrees, when plantain leaves curl and the garden wilts, and when our dogs sleep dustily in deep holes they've dug under the dogwood trees.

But with outdoor activity at a standstill, I contemplate evidence of a world still at work, the natural world that includes snakes and hornets.

There's a snake skin, six feet long or so, dangling high up in a tree in our yard.

Hornets are manufacturing a nest around a television cable under the eaves of our house.

My heat-addled brain welcomes idle speculations.

We know that black snakes climb trees, presumably sometimes to shed their skins, but we are baffled to understand how so large a snake could, have been supported by a branch as narrow and light as the one on which the skin is draped.

Did the wind blow it there from a stouter limb?

Or did the snake, in a venturesome mood, go out on a limb that swayed under its weight as it writhed its way out of its skin?

We have a live-and-let-live attitude toward black snakes, seen and unseen, but prefer them unseen. This one, at least, is safely out of sight, with its skin a mere reminder.

We've decided the best way to deal with the hornets' nest is to leave it alone until cold weather comes (if it ever does) and the hornets have left. Hornets are very aggressive if their nest is disturbed, we read in the Audubon Field Guide to North American Insects. As it is, the nest it too high up to interfere with our going in and out of the back door. The hornets crawl about the nest in a straightforward, business like way, not looking for trouble.

And if we crane our necks we can observe how the paper nest, day by day, becomes larger. To myopic eyes from the ground, the nest looks like a mound of concrete, with a round hole at the bottom. Binoculars show the papery qualities, the rough frail ridges, the overlapping layers.

There was a moment of concern about possible aggression when upstairs in the house, I heard something light batting against the outside walls. It turned out to be swarms of June bugs, noisy enough, but harmless. They seem to have spurts of activity.

Other life buzzes in our yard. Bumble bees fly low, landing on clover blossoms. Dragonflies dart. Dirt daubers daub. Butterflies flit. Grasshoppers jump.

Activity aplenty, stirred up, it seems, by the heat, while the human world is laid low.

July 14, 1993

Summer Evenings

These summer evenings, we've been sitting out on the lawn a lot, watching fireflies and listening to the cicadas.

That's what you do when you don't have air conditioning. It builds your character.

The grass is tickly and from the lawn chairs we can see assorted bugs making their way, with quiet concentration, through and over the blades. A frizzly-looking miniature grass-hopper, very green, has a weak but wicked sting.

There's a breeze of a sort, usually, and if peace doesn't come dropping slow, as in Yeat's poem, there's a close facsimile.

Children, of course, don't sit in the chairs. They roll right on that sticky grass and get up and run in all that heat, their faces red, their hair damp. That's what our children did, and we did, too, when we were children.

We caught fireflies and put them in jars. And sat on the front steps and inspected our hands. We lay on our backs and watched stars come out and swallows go down chimneys – or so it seemed. Maybe the swallows were just behind the house.

Sometimes grown-ups would point out constellations - a few, fundamental ones, and we thought how grand it would be to know them all, and got excited about the prospect, but nothing ever came of it.

Except, once, we found a book about the stars and learned dazzling facts (light years and distances), and thought we'd go about dispensing information, for a price, two pennies, to anyone who wanted to learn. No one did. I can still see the slightly puzzled look on the face on an adult neighbor up the road, when told of our proposition. Pennies were hard to come by in those days. Games on those summer evenings were "Swing the Statue" (how hilarious we thought it was to be frozen, giggling, into a stance); "Mother, may I?" (we thought we'd never forget to say "Mother, may I?", and then, inexplicably, would), and "The Big Bad Wolf." Someone would be the wolf, and hide, and the rest of us would prance about in glee, knowing soon the wolf would pounce and we would scream and run. The delicious horror. The joyful anticipation.

Our children played these same games, and different ones - Superman, with a towel-cape trailing the ground, and I don't know what else.

Children's play, I think, should not be too closely supervised. It should be a mystery to adults, the children's creation.

It should be free and idle, like summer evenings, but intense, like the throbbing of cicadas, and ecstatic – like fireflies.

July 29, 1987

Gardening

Our garden is late this year. Other people with "late" gardens are harvesting squash, but the leaves on ours are just getting to be a respectable size.

It's just as well, though, I guess. We're still eating, rather wearily, last year's squash, frozen away in the freezer.

I always think of the squash in our freezer when I think of those modern "miracles" you sometimes hear about, about unexpected guests in a poverty-stricken household being treated — to the surprise of the hosts and the gratification of all — to an unlimited supply of food (spaghetti, pork chops, whatever) from what had been thought to be a meager source. I could feed an army, I think, on the squash in our freezer, with no difficulty at all, and on short notice.

With our late garden, we've been reminded that while vegetables are sometimes slow to mature, weeds don't have this trouble. They spring up happily in all their variety and glory.

The other morning when I was doing the dishes, I sent a son out to see how the garden was getting along. He came back and said, "There are deer tracks all along the first row of the bush butterbeans, and the tops of the plants are all neatly chopped off."

Knowing his habit of exaggeration, I wasn't unduly alarmed.

"And the weeds," I said, "how are they?"

"I asked them," he replied, "and they said they are getting along very nicely, thank you."

I put down my dish towel and went out to see for myself.

Actually, I'm happy to say that the weeds in our garden are more or less under control. Some years ago, I discovered what everybody has always known, that if you tackle weeds when they're small, you can actually keep ahead of them. Not having followed this system previously, we frequently had to push through weeds to find the potatoes. Now, I pounce on weeds as soon as I can see them. I'm nearsighted, so this is not as soon as you may think, and, of course, I backslide at times, but it's wonderful how this system works. I actually like dealing with weeds when there's sure and certain hope of success. I like the sound of the chop and scrape of the hoe, and I like the feel of the finely pulverized earth. (My sons prefer the roar of the rotary tiller and the smell of gasoline fumes, but, together, we keep the garden in respectable condition.) Fighting the weeds, I maintain, is not as arduous as gathering and dealing with the produce.

Mulching is something we don't swear by. I view it with scientific interest, but some distrust. The trouble is, it covers up the soil. I like the earth, the way it feels, and the way it looks. However, I realize this could be prejudice on my part leading to deprivation for the plants involved, so we always mulch part of the garden. I put down lots of newspaper, several thicknesses, and it's a lot of trouble. You have to put down rocks too, to keep the paper from blowing away. It all looks unsightly, to my way of thinking. This year we mulched the egg plants with leaves (we have a good supply of these) and will add humus to the soil. This looks better. However, the holly leaves that got mixed up the others are a pain, if you like to walk barefoot in the garden as I do. And it was a lot of trouble carting the leaves around.

So I just can't get enthusiastic about mulching. When plants get a certain size, they provide their own shade, keeping the ground relatively moist, and relatively weed free, it seems to me. (I noticed when we were in England recently, that not one of the beautiful flower gardens we had the chance to see was mulched: I don't know about the vegetable gardens. Of course, in England, they get more rain than we do...)

I'm willing to concede that I'm wrong about mulching, that it really is as beneficial in retaining moisture and keeping down weeds as everyone says.

But I still like getting after weeds when they're small with a hoe, or pulling up by hand a satisfactorily yielding length of wire grass. (And having at my beck and call that wonderful invention, the rotary tiller.) I still like the look and feel of the uncovered earth.

August 2, 1978

Summer's End

THE poplar tree in our backyard is shedding yellow leaves onto the garage roof—confounding the painters (here, at least) who already have the heat to contend with—and signaling, however faintly, the beginning of fall.

The cicada chorus which began in July has assumed deafening proportions. The garden is beginning to give up the ghost.

But August, which can be a lovely time of changing light and subtle hints, is mugging through this year with the least amount of grace possible, slaying us with the heat, wearying us with things to do, and no energy to do them.

This is, in fact, the time of year when thou mayest in our garden behold what heat, bugs, a back and rotary tiller both out of kilter at the same time, and an absence of ten days have conspired to produce – a ragged, wilted, overgrown appearance. I feel the same way myself.

It helps to recall when the garden was neat, orderly and beautiful. Bees (with their curious combination of industry and abandon) tumbled in and out of purple snap blossoms; dew was on the broccoli. Deer tracks (but no apparent damage from deer) were visible some mornings on softly tilled earth. The garden was visited by a lizard with skin like a flame stitch needlepoint pattern – in shades of dark brown, tan and black. Now I can't see the lizard because of the weeds.

However, this weary season has compensations. One develops appreciation for vegetables scorned in the past but delighted in now because they are easy to harvest. Beets are extremely satisfactory in this respect. One tug and they're up. They don't get overripe quickly and demand instant treatment the way tomatoes do. Further, there's not another one in the same place the next day, which, of course, is the disconcerting propensity of squash and zucchini (it's been interesting to see how big zucchini will grow when given their willful way – large enough to be mistaken for watermelons, as I suspect I'm not the only one who knows).

Bugs can be viewed with philosophical calm at this point, too. It's providential that they prefer the vegetables that are hardest to gather and prepare. Just when you're sick and tired of all that stooping and picking, snapping and shelling, the bugs take over. It's a relief. However, I haven't forgiven them for destroying this year's butterbean crop before we had a decent share of it ourselves, I'm hoping a later planted row will produce enough before frost to fill the space left in the second freezer.

In fact, I find myself hoping for rain and cool so I can go out and restore some order to the garden. The rotary tiller has been fixed. My back is fine.

There's hope for the garden yet. Despite heat. Despite summer's end.

August 15, 1979

For the Record

There was a reference in the papers, again, the other day, to what I call an annoying myth about Franklin D. Roosevelt – that when he was president, the American people were ignorant of his physical condition.

Marcia Mercer, whom generally I admire, said in a column that Roosevelt, "with the complicity of the news media"... "deceived" the public about the state of his health.

I was a child and later a high school student during the four Roosevelt administrations and I knew full well that he was a cripple – and that's the word we used in those days when a spade was called a spade. Everyone knew the president was crippled, for goodness sakes.

He wasn't photographed in a wheel chair and his appearances in news reels were orchestrated to show him already standing (not being helped by aides to the microphone), or in outdoor appearances he was often seated in a car.

But this was okay with the American people. We respected (as did the press at that time) his wishes not to be photographed in ways that emphasized his handicaps. What he did and said were the important things – whether one agreed with him or not, or did or did not vote for him in each of the four presidential elections that he won.

A handicapped president today would not expect (or probably want) to receive similar treatment, and no doubt that's for the good, but to say that the public didn't know that Roosevelt couldn't walk, is a denial of the facts. People marveled that he couldn't walk; he was generally admired, and held up to school children, for going ahead with his political career despite his condition.

It may be true, as Mercer claims, that the full extent of his disability was not realized; we weren't treated to details about all the difficulties he faced, but I think Mercer erred in calling Roosevelt a "paraplegic." Photographs of the day surely show that he could stand, and a modern documentary about his condition shows how he sometimes "walked" (during his first two terms anyway) with the help of canes, ever present braces, and the close help of aides.

Being of a reticent nature myself, it pleases me somehow that Roosevelt didn't speak about his condition. He did mention it indirectly. He had no objection to being photographed at Warms Springs, Georgia, where the public knew he went for the "healing" waters. Every year, we saw him photographed with crippled children as he championed the annual March of Dimes drive to raise funds to fight polio.

I believe the only time he spoke publicly of his condition was when he addressed Congress after his return from Yalta, and spoke from a wheelchair. He apologized for not standing and mentioned the "heavy weights " on his legs. (I heard this address on a radio brought for the occasion to an assembly at my high school.)

At that time, as we now know, Roosevelt's general health was not good; he died not long afterwards. A strong case can be made that when he ran for his fourth term his health was deteriorating, and that this fact should have been revealed to the voters.

But we knew that he was "handicapped." We knew that all along.

August 22, 2001

Getting it Straight

"Beware of the time..." the sign said.

How quaint, we thought. The poet Andrew Marvell said it better, though, in the seventeenth century: "But at my back I always hear/Time's winged chariot hurrying near..."

It turned out that the sign, at the beginning of a nature trail in Chesterfield County, wasn't a philosophical meditation at all, but a warning that the gates closed at 8 o'clock.

"Beware of the time because the gates close at 8 p.m.," it said.

How quaint indeed. In fact, how ill expressed. Shouldn't the sign have said, not, "Beware of the time..." but, more tellingly, "Be aware of the time, because the gates close, etc...."? Isn't that what was meant? My husband Jack and I, who hiked on the trail recently, thought so, anyway.

We puzzled over another oddly worded admonition: "Except for fishing, collecting of plants and animals is prohibited."

With all the marvels of the Queen's English at the command of one and all, it seems strange that such a mangled construction could end up, for all to see, on a public sign. Why not: "Fishing is permitted. Do not pick plants. Leave animals alone."

The ruling was, at any rate, apparently being obeyed when we were there. We didn't see anyone collecting plants or animals (squirrels? deer? bear?); and, for that matter, we didn't see anyone "collecting" fish." Jack has now taken to saying whenever he goes fishing, "I think I'm going to collect some fish."

We don't know if any unaware or careless hikers found the gates closed.

A recently published manual on writing, by Patricia T. O'Conner, addresses, among other things, the problem of clarity, of saying what you mean. O'Conner's book is called breezily. "Words Fail Me". An apt title, but her style is a bit too breezy, and tough, for my taste. Never mind. She gives good advice on clearing up ambiguities of language.

She cites the sentence: He did not marry her because she was a Methodist.

This, she points out, could mean two things: Because she was a Methodist, he did not marry her, or. He married her, but not because she was a Methodist.

The writer should say which one he means.

Another example of a meaning mangled: Seven out of ten people are robbed by someone they know. Obviously, though it wasn't obvious to the writer, it can't be true that seven out of ten people are robbed. What was meant, notes O'Conner, is: Seven out of ten people robbed are victims of someone they know. The moral of all this, obviously, is to say what you mean.

As was pointed out in "Alice in Wonderland", saying what you mean is not the same thing as meaning what you say. The first refers to clarity, the second to sincerity, and the first is probably more important, because only when you have said exactly what you meant to say, can you know whether you want to be sincere about it.

September 6, 2000

Canning Pickles and Jam

When you make pickles, it helps to have someone around who ooh's and ah's. The same goes for jam. I always make the easy kind of pickles. I can't abide the kind to which you do something every day, without fail, for three days, or even, every hour for three hours. Get it over in one fell swoop is my motto.

This isn't meant to imply that I don't enjoy the process, because I do like the smell of spicy vinegar, the clean cut cucumber slices, the waiting glasses, hot and sparkling. But it does take a considerable block of time, and, as I said, it helps to have someone else around who also appreciates the venture.

When our children were small, our older son filled this capacity nicely. He'd linger in the kitchen, peering into the big pan on the stove, marveling as the slices converted into pickle.

"When are you going to make pickles?" he'd say each year, as the cucumbers began to abound.

This year, for the first time in a number of years, I made pickles again, and missed his company.

He was home, as it happened, the weekend I made wild plum jam. (I make jelly, rather, from the juice.) The plums are so beautiful when they fall, and the red, clear jelly is tart and delectable. My son declared he'd like to observe the jelly-making process from beginning to end.

"Why, it's simple," he said. "I thought it would be more complex."

It is simple. The only catch is that sometimes the jelly doesn't jell, and sometimes it jells itself into a rock. A purist, I frown on the use of commercial pectin, and so have to put up with the vagaries of this. My son declared himself a purist, too. "All you need is fruit, water, and sugar," he noted with interest.

The first batch turned out beautifully. Easy indeed, and what a sense of accomplishment.

But the second batch was too soft and, when reboiled, too hard. A tedious business.

For the last batch we decided to collaborate, taking turns testing the boiling liquid to see if two drops or one were forming on the edge of the spoon. I'd like to know who discovered this test, and how many gallons of jelly it took.

The rule is: When two drops of jelly form on the spoon, the soft-stage has been reached. For a firmer jelly, wait until the two drops merge into one.

A simple test, it nevertheless has uncertainties. And with two people doing the testing, the uncertainties multiply. If you tilt the spoon a certain way, it's two drops; another way, it's one. Sometimes it's one, sometimes it's two, depending upon how deeply you dip the spoon, and you can't wait forever trying to make up your mind or the liquid will boil away.

We snatched it from the heat just in time, still arguing over whether it was two drops or one, and had a jelly a bit too firm (it didn't shake in the glass the way it should) but still acceptable.

Yes, jelly making is fun. And so is making pickles. They can be pleasant solitary pursuits –but it also helps if you have company around.

September 12, 1984

Once Upon A Time

I THINK it's all right that Snow White kept house for the seven dwarfs, if that's what she wanted to do.

In all the commentary that's followed the 50th-anniversary showings this summer of the Walt Disney Snow White film, voices of radical feminists have been loud in the land.

They think it's degrading that Snow White kept house for seven men, "one of them a grump"; they think she should have had something on her mind besides waiting for her Prince to come along.

Women should be trained for jobs, in case their prince turns out to a frog, announced a letter to the New York Times, "and I expect Prince Charming to do 50 percent of the housework."

Well, I've no objections to that, but if Snow White was happy keeping house (and indications are that she was), I'm not the one to insist that she go off to the mines with the dwarfs.

Isn't choice what the women's movement is supposed to be about?

But, in case you haven't noticed, there's a movement afoot to rewrite the fairy tales, or to write new ones with a different twist.

Feminists object to the undesirable image of women created, they say, by the wicked stepmothers and witches in fairy tales.

But what about the wicked kings, the ogres and monsters, and the assorted thieves and rascals (masculine)?

The fairy tales say very strongly that evil has no gender.

They also say that evil has its consequences.

One feminist, quoted by columnist Bob Greene, has her facts all wrong. "The message of Snow White," she said, "is that looks matter a lot. All that 'Who's the fairest of them all?' stuff..."

She forgets that it was the queen who was hung up on the importance of beauty, not Snow White, and that the queen is portrayed as evil. We all know where her vanity and envy led her.

It's true that Snow White, like many a fairy tale princess, was rescued by a prince. That sounds great to me. But feminists want more activist heroines. They are writing new stories with heroines who are more adventurous and independent. That's fine – just so long as they don't change the old ones.

And they might remember, too, that it was Gretel, after all, who tricked the witch and pushed her in the oven, and that the Queen in "Rumpelstiltskin" dispatched couriers all over the kingdom to find the name of the evil dwarf. Not all fairy tale heroines languished in castles. Even Cinderella showed a lot of gumption to go off by herself in a coach.

I don't worry about the message of the fairy tales. I don't think they give children a distorted or limited view.

They teach them that evil exists, and that it can be overcome.

That's a message for all of us.

September 16, 1987

Ponies

No one rides the two ponies in our pasture very much anymore, but they are there – if not like Mt. Everest, like shaggy clumps of grass, like dandelions gone to seed.

Loving their freedom from children who hugged them, put saddles on them, or hitched them up to carts, they munch steadily away in all seasons, looking warily at anyone who gets too close, taking off lazily at the last contemptuous moment.

Once caught, though, and pressed into service for visiting children, they perform with aplomb, trotting along in a business like manner, hoping to get it over with soon, obligingly breaking into a canter when urged, and occasionally letting their feelings about the matter be known by gentle bucks and sudden stops.

Say what you will about the contrariness and intractability of ponies, I much prefer them to horses. One reason, I suppose, is because my happiness as a rider decreases the higher I get from the ground. Aloft on a horse, I feel I'm at his mercy. I not only feel it, I know it. I grow mentally weary trying to figure out what he's going to do next. When he turns his head and looks at me, I feel sure he's plotting a conspiracy. When he takes off, my heels and hands may be in the correct positions, but my heart's not in it.

With a strong little pony, it's entirely different. Just the fact that he's comfortingly close to the ground, gives me the psychological boost to have the confidence to manage him. But, of course, ponies really belong to children.

I think most people agree that ponies are more lovable than horses. I'd be hard put to estimate how many kisses have been placed on "Nannie Goat's" fuzzy nose. Our pony, "Nannie Goat", so called because with her whiskers, yellow eyes, and trim little hooves, she does look something like a little goat, was a frequent winner in the costume classes of gymkhanas put on by the children. Short, fat, and cream colored, she has pulled a "peddler" in a cart (a straw hat on her head), or borne an excited "gypsy" in a long dress (flowers in her mane) to the judges' stand to receive blue ribbons.

"Puggy" is a plucky little black pony with a wickedly fast canter. This made her lots of fun on trail rides. But Nannie Goat, pulling a cart that I've seen many times disappear on one wheel around a curve in a road in the woods with a child bouncing wildly on it, could usually keep up with her. She couldn't stand being left behind.

Puggy learned to jump and even seemed to enjoy it. Nannie Goat refused every jump with supercilious indifference.

In the way of ponies, they are inseparable, and also stay close to the horses, "Hope" and "Surprise". Sometimes the cat joins them in the barn.

I'm sure there are lots of ponies like ours around — part of the landscape, and part of people's lives.

Now that it's getting colder, the ponies are growing their thick winter coats. Nannie Goat especially gets a very furry look. On cold winter mornings, her fur will bristle out all over her, like a halo.

    I just remembered that a Brownie troop is coming here next week for a nature walk. Part of the walk will be gathering locusts seed pods to feed to the ponies. The ponies will be grateful for the food, and will tolerate all the attention and admiration.
    Who knows? Maybe they miss it.

October 10, 1977

For the Picking...

Autumn wouldn't be autumn without apples.

I don't know much about varieties of apples, except that Delicious apples aren't delicious.

"Get non-Delicious apples," I always specify when handing over a grocery list to my husband.

Winesaps cook well, I do know, and are usually what we buy.

Friends in Washington State, where Delicious apples abound, also sigh about the lack of taste and poor texture of the variety. They were developed to stand up well under shipping, they say, and that they may do.

The names of apples are delightful. Winesap, Jonathan, York Imperial, Rome Beauty, Rhode Island Greening.

But the apples that are the staple of our autumn days are nameless.

They grow on two trees in our pasture where an aged pony also takes an interest in them. Volunteer apple trees aren't always the best.

Johnny Appleseed notwithstanding, trees grown from seed usually don't reproduce true to type. The fruit can turn out knobby, hard, misshapened, and undistinguished in taste.

Our pasture apples are volunteers, but fortunately are good when cooked.

We've had even better trees in the past (nursery stock), but they were planted long ago by previous owners of our place, and in the way of all apple trees, they grew gnarled, spare, and succumbed. The trees we've planted to replace them aren't producing yet.

So it's to the pasture we go on bright autumn days and misty, to knock down apples with a long cedar stick, to hear them pounding to the ground, and then to pick them up, amid the grass and scattered leaves, to dump in a cardboard box.

There's always a path around the trees that the pony and wilder animals have made. I don't know that our free apples are such an economy. They take a lot of sugar in cooking. But like Mt. Everest, they are there. I cook and freeze large quantities.

The trees are lovely to look at. One with yellow-green apples; the other, with smaller, red ones. We never spray any of the trees. Too much trouble, bad for the ecology, and what's wrong with an imperfect apple.

Gathered on an autumn day, they are perfect enough.

October 4, 1989

Raw Materials

It's a pride of lions, and a gaggle of geese. I've been wondering what you'd call a lot of stones.

Oodles of rocks? Masses of granite? They've been accumulating in our backyard. Our older son is building a low stone wall for us, to enclose and define part of the yard.

We're very pleased about the project – even if there is something that doesn't love a wall. In New England it's mostly the frozen-ground-swell that's a wall's enemy. Here, it's likely to be honeysuckle, just waiting to get a running start to take over and obliterate. But we're willing to risk it, for the sake of the solidity and beauty of a wall of stone.

It will go by a walnut tree, and, already, the combination of the dark trunk, the compound leaves of the tree, and the shapes and shadows of the stone, strewn now on the grass, is very pleasing.

The stones are coming from the far flung corners of the yard. At one time there apparently were a number of small structures on the property with stone foundations, and stones are lying loosely about, or sometimes not so loosely. Richard ferrets them out and transports them to the site of the wall. "How he move that?" asked our cleaning lady one day when she looked out and saw a particularly big rock on the lawn.

That one weighed about 500 pounds, we estimated. What we did was pry it up with a metal rod used as a lever over a smaller rock. I say "we". My job was gingerly placing bricks underneath as the rock was gradually lifted from its resting position and turned on another side. Once, I applied my weight to the lever and was amazed to be an almost effortless part of a basic principle of physics that works so astoundingly. I understand how they must have felt after they built Stonehenge.

After the rock was flipped (ha) a sufficient number of times to get it away from surrounding vines and trees, Richard, using the lever, got it up on a wooden sled he'd built for the purpose and chained the sled to the back of the pickup truck. From there it was smooth sailing – until the ordeal of getting the rock off the sled and on the ground again. He enjoys the work.

All the rocks aren't that big. Some he has been able to lift onto a wheelbarrow and trundle across the yard, but there are a number of satisfyingly big ones. It will be a wall without mortar, a dry wall. It will be about 40 feet long, and about three feet high, with part of it in the ground, for solidity. The top will be flat, so we can sit on it on autumn days, or whenever. There will be a gate, or rather, just an open space, so we can get easily to the orchard and compost heap beyond, though, for a while, we considered making the wall intact, so we could leap over it, on these journeys, for exercise.

Some of the rocks will have to be cut, and the positions of all thought out and planned. Richard has goggles, a mallet, a chisel, and a degree in fine arts from the Rhode Island School of Design.

We're expecting a great wall.

October 25, 1984

A Voting Record

WHEN my 81-year-old mother votes in the November 4 election, she will be one of that stalwart band of women — how many are there now, I wonder — who have voted in every presidential election since women first received the vote.

Troy Saul had just turned 21 in Waynesboro, Mississippi, when in November 1920, following ratification of the 19th Amendment by a sufficient number of states, women in the United States were permitted to vote for president.

She cast her vote then for the Democratic ticket headed by James M. Cox, with Franklin D. Roosevelt as running mate.

The news that the Republicans carried the day and Warren G. Harding was elected president was duly reported in the Wayne County (Mississippi) News, edited by my father George Kilpatrick.

My mother, with one exception, has continued to vote the Democratic ticket ever since. She believes the Democratic Party is more responsive to the needs of the people, she says; and the fact that her three children, and their spouses, have almost always voted for the Republican candidates, has not swayed her in her beliefs.

She has always been avidly interested in national politics.

When she married and moved to Virginia where my father had bought the "Brunswick Times-Gazette" in Lawrenceville, she listened with him to the news of the 1924 election of Calvin Coolidge on a crystal radio set with earphones.

Later, after his death, and in the 40's and 50's with her second husband, the late John Fraunces McCurley, who also edited the "Gazette", she never missed election returns on radio. Now, grandchildren come to her house to watch elections on television.

She says she grew up in a family interested in politics. A grandfather subscribed to three daily newspapers, *Memphis Commercial Appeal, New Orleans Times Picayune,* and *Atlanta Constitution.* The first president she remembers hearing her parents and grandparents discuss was Theodore Roosevelt (1901-1908) She also remembers "Mr. Taft" and "Mr. Wilson".

All presidents, and indeed all presidential candidates, are always called "Mister" by my mother. It's never "Reagan" or "Carter" or "Anderson," but "Mr. Reagan," "Mr. Carter," "Mr. Anderson." Eisenhower, of course, was never "Ike" or even "General Eisenhower." but always "Mr. Eisenhower." In the past, she referred to "Mr. Truman," "Mr. Hoover," "Mr. Coolidge".

She admired President Woodrow Wilson very much, although she was too young to vote for him and women did not then have the vote. He was also admired by her father. My brother, Allen Wilson Kilpatrick (also a "Gazette" editor) was named for him. The one time my mother did not vote for the Democratic candidate was in 1972 when she voted for the Republican candidate, Richard Nixon. "I'll never do that again," she says emphatically, "That Mr. Nixon!"

During the 1976 campaign, my mother was teased by a son-in-law because her candidate had granted Playboy magazine an interview. (My mother has unequivocal views; when she saw the movie *Love Story* some years back, she walked out, demanded the usher take her to the manager and demanded, and received, her money back.) In this instance, however, she had a ready answer. "I'm not voting for the candidate," she said firmly. "I'm voting for the party."

No one can say, of course, which party will win the 1980 election. or which candidate, "Mr. Carter," "Mr. Reagan," or "Mr. Anderson," but on November 4, 60 years after she first voted for a president, I will be driving my mother to the polls.

It will be a privilege.

October 29, 1980

A Question of Time

MISS MANNERS, whom I have always trusted (and I'm not sure I've used that "whom" correctly) to give sensible advice about correct social behavior, amazed me the other day with some outrageous advice.

I think it's outrageous. She admitted it was a rule (did she call it a rule?) most people have forgotten.

This was in her newspaper column in which her wit and skill in language are sometimes matched by that of the people who write in to her with questions about delicate situations.

Someone wanted to know if indeed it is incorrect to wear a wristwatch at a social event in the evening.

And indeed it is incorrect, says Miss Manners.

I don't know that I'm going to read Miss Manners anymore if she's going to go around giving advice like that.

Her rationale is that to wear a wristwatch indicated that you're mindful of the time (and who isn't) and that the absence of a wristwatch is a charming gesture indicating that you're going to have a perfectly lovely time at this event planned by your charming host and hostess, without ever a thought to time. But what if you have a baby sitter? a young friend of mine queried.

And what if you merely want to know what time it is? What's wrong with that?

I don't think the charming host and hostess who, of course, besides not wearing wristwatches either, don't have a clock within viewing distance of their guests, who are having such a wonderful time, would like it very much if none of their guests ever departed because they didn't know what time it was.

What would Cinderella have done if that clock hadn't started striking?

Ah, but Miss Manners has an answer here, and this is where she is doubly disappointing. A gentleman is allowed to have a watch, she says, provided it's the kind that fits in the little pocket in his suit manufactured for that purpose, and ladies are advised to carry wristwatches discreetly in their purses.

What hypocrisy. What dishonesty. Are you supposed to be having a good time, without ever a thought to time, or are you not?

I think a room full of ladies opening their purses and gentlemen pulling out watches is no indication of anyone having a good time at all, when it's much easier, simpler, and quicker to take a quick look at your wrist while you're having a perfectly wonderful time but don't want to overstay your visit — or you're having a horrible time and want to leave after a decent interval, and what's wrong with that?

Miss Manners, whom I have always enjoyed reading (and again I'm not sure about that "whom") has gone too far here.

November 11, 1993

Time for the Feast

TRUE Indian summer comes after a frost in November (not in October). Traditionally it was a time when Indians went on the warpath, though why anyone would want to fight in such a glorious weather is beyond me.

Anyway, after Indian summer comes Thanksgiving. Here it is, already upon us. Sometimes Indian summer will extend or skip to Thanksgiving, with youngsters playing in leaves after the feast and grown-ups going jacketless on long walks; but I can remember some cold, cold Thanksgivings.

That's the kind celebrated in "Over the River and Through the Woods to Grandfather's House We Go." Maybe there should be new songs for the season about driving through the city to Grandmother's condominium. If I were Ogden Nash, I could think of something to rhyme with condominium. And maybe some songs about warmer Thanksgivings. What rhymes with "global warming"?

Grateful am I this Thanksgiving that the children have said they'll do all the cooking. Preparing Thanksgiving dinner has long been a favorite activity of mine, but never say I don't like change. The first time, several years ago, that the children took over, they complained that I kept peeping into the kitchen. No more.

Others can contend with the fact that as one wit observed, the chicken, and by extension, most certainly the turkey, was not designed for cooking — it's hard to get all of it all done without getting some of it dry.

Someone else can set the table(s), too, hoping that all the dishes will hide the fact that Grandmother (me) didn't iron the tablecloths. The silver will be polished; though, I hope, as I write this, there's still time.

There are those who, for large family gatherings, go in for handsome paper plates and plastic flat ware of the sturdier variety. They have a point. But I still like bringing out the finery. Alas, we don't use it often. Thanksgiving is the time. It will be interesting to see if the children in future years hold to this theory. So far, they do.

An ornery Thanksgiving task, always designated to the children, is to bring in chairs from other rooms, for dining. This requires some judicious planning. That chair that's especially wobbly shouldn't go to the hefty uncle. And this year, where to fit in the baby's high chair? Actually, it's not a high chair. It's a low chair, with a tray, that fits onto an ordinary chair. Oh the marvels of modern ingenuity.

Babies of the modern age still toss to the rug at random food that's on the way to their mouths. I think I'll put a towel under the bottom-tier chair.

As a child I liked making place cards for Thanksgiving, though really I made them only once, cards with a stand-up haystack and colored pumpkins going by directions from Wee Wisdom. My mother saved them, and we used them again and again, erasing, as time went by, the name of long widowed Aunt Mattie, who at age 65 remarried and celebrated elsewhere, and writing in the name of "Charles," the new beau and eventual husband of Aunt Ima. It would be fun if those cards were still extant. Never mind. A few years ago a great-niece (I forget which one) brought us a great supply of "turkeys," made in kindergarten from walnuts and pipe cleaners. What an ingenious and patient kindergarten teacher she must have had. I'll distribute these colorful birds around the table again, for guests to admire anew. Newlyweds, from Oregon, will be at the Thanksgiving feast this year; the brother, and sister-in-law of our older son's wife. Thanksgiving will be a blessed event. It always is. Thank God.

November 21, 2001

Giving Thanks

Like Miss Manners, I sometimes like to give out rules. The subject today is thank-you notes.

Some people don't write them, but this advice is for considerate, appreciative people who do.

Since December rivals June for weddings, these rules apply especially to thank-you notes for wedding gifts.

Rule No. One.

Watch your grammar.

I couldn't believe it when a bride, with a brand new college degree, thanked me "so much for the fork in our silver pattern that you gave Adolphus and I."

I wanted to snatch it back from Adolphus and she.

Rule No. Two.

Repetition is unnecessary.

How many notes, after the first paragraph of adequate and often lavish thanks, conclude with the sentence, "I want to thank you again, etc., etc.,"?

Once is really enough.

Rule No. Three.

If you don't like a gift, don't say so.

You wouldn't think a rule like this would be necessary, and true, I've never received the equivalent of the legendary note written by the little girl to her aunt: "Thank you very much for the pin cushion. I've always wanted a pin cushion, but not very much." But faint praise can cut.

I once bought a crystal ashtray for a wedding gift. (Both the bride and groom smoked, and this was before smoking was suspect, so that's not the issue.) It was a simple gift, but I thought the crystal was handsome.

When I was making my purchase, another customer was buying a present for the same couple. She chose a silver wine cooler, engraved. She's a closer friend of the bride, I told myself. And she was. Still, the bride, in her note, thanked me for "that" ashtray (not the lovely ashtray or even the crystal ashtray, but "that" ashtray), and I felt my gift was being belittled. So, if you don't like a gift, please don't say so.

Rule No. Four.

I always like it when a gift of money is answered with a note of thanks that mentions what the money is being used for. This isn't necessary, of course, but it's interesting. "We're putting the money toward the purchase of our bed," or "toward restoring the antique silver teapot Aunt Henrietta gave us."

(On second thought, maybe that wouldn't be appreciated by Aunt Henrietta.)

Rule No Five (not really a rule).

I also like it when, for a change, the groom writes the note. "Marcia is preparing to defend her PhD dissertation," one groom felt it necessary to explain.

Rule No. Six (a continuation of Rule No. Five).

Any hints of the life the couple is leading adds immeasurably to a thank-you note. Whether it's:

"We're off to Brussels next week where John will be with the Embassy for the next two years, and I'll be working on my novel."

Or: "We're settling down on the hog farm."

Both are of interest to the gift giver who, after all, by giving a gift, indicated a kind of interest in, and best wishes for, the couple's future.

December 4, 1999

Communicating

WHEN I read articles about "Communicating Skills for Couples," I marvel that our marriage has lasted 37 years.

We never talk the way the people in those articles do. Or rather, the way the authors of the articles say that people should talk to insure domestic tranquility...

I wonder if anyone talks that way. Is it all a delusion of the authors?

The other morning, not long ago, I was reading a communicating skills article, and looked up to see my husband coming into the kitchen with muddy boots.

"What I'm supposed to say to you," I commented carefully, "according to this article on communicating skills..."

"Article on what?" my husband said. "Don't mumble."

"Communicating skills," I repeated. "This article says I'm not supposed to say to you, 'You're tracking mud on the floor again.' I'm supposed to say, 'It makes me feel unhappy when you track mud on the floor.' "

"My reply to that," said my husband, sitting down to take off his boots, which is what he always does when he tracks mud on the floor, "is that it makes me unhappy when you talk in that artificial way."

Exactly. What's wrong with a little honest bickering.

The theory of the communicating-skills people is that you should avoid accusations and statements that put blame on the other person. The other person, then, doesn't feel defensive and is more apt to do what you want.

That's what I call maneuvering.

And the trouble with maneuvering is that if it's done too often, too persistently, and too skillfully, or even if it's done at all, the person who is being maneuvered usually catches on to it. You don't have to be very smart to do this.

And who likes to be maneuvered? What sort of domestic tranquility is that?

Children are very good at catching on to maneuvering. In a children's book by Lois Lowry, a mother who doesn't want her five-year-old to take his bear to the park, says to him, "Your bear has a cold, I think. I heard him coughing this morning. He really should stay home in bed." "No," replied the child, "I gave him penicillin."

That child could write a book on communicating skills.

For when the communicating-skills people say, "communicating skills," they frequently mean maneuvering skills.

They should come right out and call their articles, "Maneuvering Skills for Couples," and see how many takers there are.

Call a spade a spade. That's what they should do.

December 30, 1987

Winter Mornings

Pink is not my favorite color, except on early winter mornings when pink is in the eastern sky. Then it's breathtaking – like clouds of breath on the cold air.

Below the pink clouds are blue ones, and they stretch the sky out to unbelievable proportions. Not, however, like the imagery in T. S. Elliot's poem: *Let us go then, you and I, when the evening is spread out against the sky. Like a patient etherized upon a table...* I agree, rather, with C. S. Lewis in his poem:

> I am so coarse, the things the poets see
> Are obstinately invisible to me.
> For twenty years I've stared my level best
> To see if evening — any evening — would suggest
> A patient etherized upon a table;
> In vain. I simply wasn't able.

Anyway, they are both talking about the evening sky. And it's the morning ones that have been taking my breath these wintry days when our almanac calendar says the sun has been getting up at 6:57, 6:58, 6:59, then a long stretch when it gets up at seven, and a minute later, day by day (the very heart of winter) until, suddenly, bang, on January 9, it's due to rise one minute earlier than the

7:14 of the morning before, and we're on our way to spring. (Beginning at Christmas, of course, the crucial date, the days have already been getting longer in the afternoons.)

I'd just as soon stay in winter for a while, when the sun and I get up at about the same time, and I can see what's going on in the morning sky.

The pink fades, by the time I've got the coffee perking, to cream and yellow, and then it's dispelled into the clear light of a December day.

The light and space of winter are its greatest attractions, for me, anyway. Trees stand out singly and brightly. The sky is enormous. Grasses are laid low, heavy with frost. You can see through the bare trees to fields you only suspected were there.

I think one reason my husband likes winter mornings so much is because I cook hot cereal – oatmeal and cream of wheat (comforting names for comforting substances). I enjoy this too, Also, the fireplace fire, which he likes to keep going and provide for, really makes an early difference in a room in which the thermostat has been set at 50 degrees overnight. That's what the thermostat says; I haven't the heart to look at the thermometer. I'd rather just look at the fire, giving out its glow.

Winter is a time, I think, when despite our modern homes and conveniences, we're aware of threats to our safety. Winter reminds us that danger and difficulties exist. In winter, we have to take our comforts where we find them — like birds flurrying within the shelter of a cedar tree or clinging for a moment, windblown, to the rim of a bird feeder — and there's pleasure and courage in that.

December 26, 1979

Water Trouble

CHRISTMAS this year was a calamitous season at our house. In addition to the usual stresses and strains, this year we had a driver's license renewal, car inspections, license tag replacements, and our Christmas tree fell down three times.

The last time, we heaved it back up and let the decorations fall where they may; it's too much trouble to decorate a tree three times.

Also, our water pipes froze, one burst, and the water pump decided it had had enough of the whole weary mess and had to be over-hauled and rehabilitated at considerable trouble and expense.

If I ever build another house, which is doubtful, my first and prime specification will be a house in which the pipes never freeze. This seems a simple requirement in this day of technological miracles. I'm sure there are already people in the land living in homes where pipes don't freeze, but we have never been among those happy few.

A lot of literature is written nowadays about how Christmas doesn't live up to people's expectations and therefore causes depression instead of euphoria. My Christmas expectations are very simple — freely flowing water when you turn on the spigot.

However, I refuse to be downcast when this doesn't occur. Christmas, above all, is a time of hope.

Friends tell us there are all sorts of tricks you can employ to keep water from freezing: keep a slight stream of water flowing from a spigot at all times; or put a portable electric heater in the basement near the pipes, or near the water pump.

Somehow, there must be a deep Puritan strain in me that deplores waste, because I just can't go to bed happy if the water is running. I guess, irrational as it is, I'd just rather wake up and find the pipes frozen. Maybe I can overcome this.

As for a heater in the basement, we don't have a basement, and our pump house (a gazebo-like affair, with solid walls) is inhabited by rats (and snakes if it gets warm enough) that just might, I fear, in a careless moment knock the heater over. Someone suggested that we heat rocks instead and put these, overnight, in the pump house near the engine. A happy idea, I thought.

I was lifting the first of two big rocks into the oven (350 degrees for 45 minutes, I had decided) when a son said apprehensively, "Do those rocks weigh more than a turkey? You might break the stove rack." The obvious solution which I should have thought of in the first place, in view of the energy crisis, was to place the rocks in the fireplace. They soon were toasty warm and we hastily transferred them in metal buckets to the pump house. That night was warmer anyway, so it may have been labor in vain, but shall keep this method in mind for another sub-freezing night.

(I should point out that we take other precautions also. The tank in the pump house is wrapped cozily in fiberglass insulation, looking like a giant tea-cozy, and the pipes under our house are insulated too, but we have a northern exposure that wreaks havoc with the best insulated pipes of man. At least, it does in the South, where houses usually aren't built, alas, with deep freezes in mind.)

Of course, when you haven't had running water for 24 hours or more, there's great rejoicing when it finally comes trickling and spitting and gushing out of the spigot. You realize how right St. Francis was to say that "our Sister Water" is "precious", and "pure" and "good". He might also have said "temperamental," but it's a very welcome commodity.

We had hoped, that with all the frozen water in the pipes, the water in our pond would freeze too; enough, at least, for ice skating. No such luck, however. "Temperamental," I think, is the word for water.

December 30, 1980

Moving the Millstone

We're starting the New Year by already having moved... literally a millstone.

A millstone is not an easy object to move.

We wish we knew the history of the granite stone that's been in our front yard longer than any of us can remember... what mill it came from, and what river, and how it ended up here. It's an especially large stone, 53 inches in diameter, nine inches thick; and we've liked having it, flat, in the yard where, on occasion we would sit, or, passing, just admire.

Our son has now moved it twelve feet, all estimated 2424 pounds of it, to get it away from an encroaching oak, and to place it at a more visible spot, the better to see, and admire, and sit upon. We think it's a beautiful stone. The center has an opening that's shaped, more or less, like a Celtic cross, and lines cut into the stone make an interesting pattern.

Richard moved it by using as a lever a metal rod and a rock, and gradually shifting it along. At one point, at his urging, I pushed down on the rod myself "to see how easy it is." I couldn't believe what little effort it took to lift the edge of the stone from the ground. In Physics 101 when I drew diagrams of levers, I'd really had no idea of the marvels of physics.

It wasn't all as easy as pie, of course. The rock placed under the lifted edge had to be moved from spot to spot as the stone gradually moved in the direction opposite to the way the rod was being pushed. By the time the stone was moved to its ultimate destination, it had made a revolution of 360 degrees.

To begin with, it had been covered with thick ivy vines which my son pulled off; soil had to be dug out in places so the stone could more easily move. The entire operation took most of an afternoon. Richard, who teaches math a Wake Forest, estimated the stone's considerable weight by first measuring and weighing a small granite rock and determine that eight cubic inches of that type granite weighed a pound. By mathematical formula using the millstone's radius and involving π (which I learned about in the fifth grade but have never understood) he calculated the volume of the millstone, at 19,393.43 cubic inches. He then divided this by eight.

The over-a-ton stone, in its new location, is now resplendent in the winter sun. We expect to enjoy it in all seasons.

We're also enjoying a brick sidewalk to our front porch that we'd practically forgotten about, so long had the walk been covered with moss and grass. Most of the time we use the back entrance to rural house, and most guests do, too, since the location of the driveway makes this easier. I'd prefer using the front door all the time, but it doesn't work out that way. From time to time I've made efforts to keep clear the 44-by-5 foot sidewalk at the front, but moss has galloped in and tough grass invaded.

Imagine our delight, then, when, in, what was almost like an archaeological dig, the rosy brick appeared again, in its herringbone pattern, as our son peeled away layers of moss and pulled up the grass.

A good New Year's Resolution will be to try to keep the walk the way it is now.

December 30, 1998

Breaks

COLLEGE students of the male sex, between the time they first leave home and the date of graduation, develop a capacity to eat everything in sight, as well as all the groceries stashed away for a week, when they come home for what is called a "break."

"Break" is a good word. It just about breaks the parent or parents who may be financing the grocery buying, and it almost surely breaks down the parent or parents who are doing the cooking.

I can't believe our two sons ate with such thorough determination and with such wide, eclectic taste when they lived with us full-time.

One of them admitted as much.

"It's free," he said, taking out the remnants of a ham, and discarding a turkey carcass. At college, he had had an unexpected taste of doing some of his own shopping and cooking, and now has a sudden, exhilarated appreciation for the home refrigerator.

The other son, also a part-time cook, likes the vegetables that come out of the home freezer. Three varieties per meal.

Bleakly, I watch what would last my husband and me for a week of dinners disappear at one sitting.

The boys when at home cook their own breakfast and lunch (and clean up afterwards), and this, at least, is a help to the home cook. Or is it? Eggs by the dozen and cheese by the pound are transformed into breakfast omelets. Hamburgers and milk are devoured at noon as if there is no tomorrow. The boys are also fond of between-meal snacks. A gallon of my homemade soup is heated up at three o'clock in the afternoon. The smell of cheese toast, or of hot dogs and coleslaw comes wafting from the kitchen at ten at night. During the recent Christmas break, I took to writing neat little notes, "Save this for Tuesday's dinner," and putting them around in the ice box.

Dinners, which since the boys had gone to college had become little gems of meals, or so I fancied, had to be expanded info vast and plenteous repasts.

Any notion that any of the roast chickens, stuffed potatoes with cheese, and the requisite three vegetables spread out so bounteously on the table would survive to form the basis for another meal disappeared the first night the boys were home. I thought with wonder of the stamina of my Grandmother Kilpatrick and my Grandmother Saul, with six, and four, sons, respectively, to feed. I thought of farm wives of the past cooking noon-day meals not only for their families, but for an army of "hands."

By comparison, I suppose I've had an easy time of it.

And the boys have been good company, pleasant to have around (for the most part). They have performed useful tasks in the house and yard. (I wish I'd gotten them to perform more). They are at the point of making plans for their future, and it's exciting to be in on this.

And now they are back at college.

What a break.

January 12, 1983

Yesteryear's Snows

It's impossible not to think of your childhood when it snows; snow in the life of children is such a pervadingly delightful event, looked forward to, thought about, reveled in when present, and regretted when vanished. Has there ever been a child that didn't like snow?

What children never get over, being so new to snow, is its wonder: that all those individual snowflakes cluttering the air and landing on eyelashes can end up massed together transforming the world. But, being pragmatists, children also give equal billing to the things you can do in snow, the varied types of play and fun available only when snow lies on the ground. This is as good as the magic.

Remembering snows of my childhood, I remember entire afternoons, or mornings if school was out, spent hurling and plunging onto snow. Even if we went inside for a while, for a rest and a change, there was the bright, cozy awareness of the snow outside, waiting.

"Little children just don't like snow," the father of a childhood friend used to say to us when it snowed. He was as much a child (at heart) as we, and, as he said this, had a happy, knowing smile just waiting to be rebutted.

"Oh, don't you wish it would hurry up and melt?" he'd say. We protested heartily, safe in the knowledge of his good will, happy to have an adult who would engage in such a serious argument, and convinced that we could win, with our logic, any debate about the merits of snow.

Remembering childhood snows, one remembers, too, the shouts that accompanied the play, and the smell of woolen gloves, steaming in rows on radiators in school classrooms. The gloves and our woolen snow pants, worn in those days over dresses and pulled off once we went inside, got caked and matted with snow during recess. While the gloves steamed, the baggy snow pants, dark blue or brown, hung in the cloakroom under coats that dripped melting snow onto the galoshes on the floor. The galoshes were troublesome; hard to put on, hard to buckle, button or snap. Also difficult were the snow pants' elastic foot straps, frequently icy and wet, that had to be slipped on under our shoes before the struggle with galoshes began. But bundled in wool, fortified by rubber, never dreaming of synthetics, we kept warm.

All these clothes went on and off repeatedly on school days, with amazing rapidity, for Big Recess in the morning, for Lunch Hour which lasted an hour and again for Little Recess in the afternoon. Maybe we stayed inside sometimes at school during recess when there was snow, but I don't remember it. Having others to play with increased the compulsion to run out. We made snowmen despite the fact that the trampling feet left few areas where we could gather snow. In groups we rolled wobbly, giant snowballs that gathered dirt and debris as we pushed and rolled.

Recesses lasted longer then, but too soon, the bell rang and we would herd jovially back into the building, with snuffling noses, the red cheeks I notice now on children in the snow, and toes that were beginning to curl with cold. Then the great unbundling and pulling off of snowsuits, the reaching for hangers in the cloakroom began again.

The darkness of the schoolroom (and our homes) after we had been out in the brightness of the snow was always a surprise. Our tolerant teachers listened unwearyingly to our cries of amazement, and while the radiators popped and steamed, led us slowly back to lessons.

January 23, 1980

A Modest Proposal

I OFFER a simple solution to a complex problem. Would that it were really simple, and that it would work. There is no guarantee.

Put school desks in rows facing the teacher's desk, and nail the desks to the floor. I can't say that discipline problems in schools would instantly disappear and that academic performance would improve, but this arrangement might help. It's worth a try.

On TV documentaries about classes and schools, the classrooms, almost always, are an assortment of tables in an informal but studied array, with students facing each other rather than the teacher, and with the teacher a free spirit wandering about the area.

The goal of this set-up, I suppose, is a sense of community and cooperation in learning.

But...to watch the teacher, students have to turn or twist around in their chairs; written class work is performed elbow to elbow with other students, and oh the distracting noise of scraping chairs when students move their seats.

I think it is perfectly obvious that pupils seated at tables find it easier to talk, whisper and giggle, to copy from each other's papers, and to evade the attention of the teacher.

On the other hand, the once common arrangement of nailed down desks in rows, all facing the teacher's desk permanently at the front of the room, is an arrangement that suggests order, authority, and concentration. I would say that these are elements essential to learning. (I don't think it a sin for a teacher to be a figure of authority.) There are other factors that help learning, but these are basic.

The teacher, naturally, is free to move about the room, to inspect students' work, to give extra help, or just for a change, but the teacher's desk, at the front, remains the focal point of the classroom. Like the hearth in a home, like a lighthouse on the shore.

Students are encouraged to stay put. They have a clear view of the teacher, and the blackboards, and videos. Their line of vision isn't blocked by other students. Not in close proximity to others, they aren't as easily distracted (let us hope).

And show me the child who doesn't like a desk of his own. It's his own territory, his space. It can improve that vaunted sense of self esteem. He is separate from everyone else. He (or she) can spread his arms across his desk without bumping into a neighbor; he can wiggle or fidget in his seat without jostling others. His desk offers a needed haven.

I know, of course, that schools reflect society and that society today is vastly different from the way it was forty or fewer years ago, and that consequently schools face problems not previously known.

But a practice from the past might possibly be a help in the present

January 30, 2002

Perils

WITH our microwave oven out of order, our household has reverted to what now seem Neanderthal practices.

Water is boiled in a kettle for coffee or tea; leftovers are heated in the conventional stove oven; eggs and bacon are prepared in a skillet. Hardships. Hardships. Hardships.

The repair man said it would be cheaper to buy a new microwave than to repair this one, and as difficult as it is for the Depression-era generation to accept this, cavalier philosophy, we've decided to abide by the repair man's judgment. Not without sorrow. As Beatrix Potter said of Peter Rabbit, "It was the second little jacket he'd lost in a fortnight," and this will be the second microwave oven we've bought in two years.

At first, my husband Jack, being of a frugal nature, suggested we might get by with the old one a while longer. While it has now twice uttered a guttural noise, and emitted flashes of light, at other times when we forget and automatically put in a cup of water, the microwave has behaved properly.

It might be like our toaster, Jack pointed out. We've been getting along with an old toaster and that's only partially operative. (It toasts just one side of the bread and doesn't pop up) We've trained ourselves to regulate it.

Still, a microwave oven with occasional flashes of light and guttural sounds is more alarming than burnt toast. We've both agreed we need a new one. We had no sooner reached this decision than our dishwasher (relatively new) leaked water all over the kitchen floor. Troubles never come singly, etc. Our friendly electrician (whose late father I knew in the grammar grades – as elementary schools were quaintly called in those days) will come to our aid soon I hope.

It makes me wonder what is going to break down next. Our refrigerator has some age on it, as the saying goes. The washing machine gets heavy duty when our grandchild visits, but so far is holding up. My computer hums along nicely.

Fortunately, we don't have a dryer that may go awry. I know there are those who consider hanging clothes outdoors on a line a Neanderthal practice, but this has worked very well for us. Solar energy saves a lot of money, and I like to see the clothes flapping in the wind...

"But what do you do when it rains?" I'm asked.

I cope as people in Neanderthal times did: I drape wet clothes over shower rods, or wait until the sun shines. I'm reminded, in this connection, of a maid-of-all-work we once had who would cheerfully announce, "I'll wash tomorrow, do it don't rain." A good philosophy.

I digress. But no, I think I've said all I intended to, on perils of the technological age.

February 6, 2002

Georgia as a teenager.

Georgia in the mid 1950's, probably at Shelby Farm.

Georgia and her mother Troy Saul Kilpatrick McCurley, 1984.

Georgia and Jack at Sherwood, 2001. (Photo by Donna Schatz.)

www.ingramcontent.com/pod-product-compliance
Lightning Source LLC
Chambersburg PA
CBHW060815050426
42449CB00008B/1673